Contents

Poems

'Lines Written in Early Spring' by William Wordsworth	4
'England in 1819' by Percy Bysshe Shelley	8
'Shall earth no more inspire thee' by Emily Brontë	12
'In a London Drawingroom' by George Eliot	16
'On an Afternoon Train from Purley to Victoria, 1955' by James Berry	20
'Name Journeys' by Raman Mundair	24
'pot' by Shamshad Khan	28
'A Wider View' by Seni Seneviratne	34
'Homing' by Liz Berry	38
'A century later' by Imtiaz Dharker	42
'The Jewellery Maker' by Louisa Adjoa Parker	46
'With Birds You're Never Lonely' by Raymond Antrobus	50
'A Portable Paradise' by Roger Robinson	56
'Like an Heiress' by Grace Nichols	60
'Thirteen' by Caleb Femi	64

Comparison

Comparing Poetry	68
Comparison Grid	72
Practice Questions	73

The Exam

Tips and Assessment Objectives	78
Planning a Poetry Response	80
Grade 5 Annotated Response	82
Grade 7+ Annotated Response	84

Glossary 86

Answers 91

Lines Written in Early Spring
by William Wordsworth

I heard a thousand blended notes,
While in a grove I sate reclined,
In that sweet mood when pleasant thoughts
Bring sad thoughts to the mind.

5 To her fair works did Nature link
The human soul that through me ran;
And much it grieved my heart to think
What man has made of man.

Through primrose tufts, in that green bower,
10 The periwinkle trailed its **wreaths;**
And 'tis my faith that every flower
Enjoys the air it breathes.

The birds around me hopped and played,
Their thoughts I cannot measure:—
15 But the least motion which they made
It seemed a thrill of pleasure.

The budding twigs spread out their fan,
To catch the breezy air;
And I must think, do all I can,
20 That there was pleasure there.

If this belief from heaven be sent,
If such be Nature's holy plan,
Have I not reason to lament
What man has made of man?

How to use your Snap Revision Text Guide

This 'Worlds and Lives' Snap Revision Guide will help you to get a top mark in the poetry anthology section of your AQA English Literature exam. It is divided into clear sections so you can easily find help with different poems or specific exam skills. This book covers everything you will need to know for the exam:

The poems: a detailed analysis of all fifteen 'Worlds and Lives' poems, covering themes, context, poetic voice, and the effects of language, structure and form.

Comparison: how to come up with ideas and structure a comparison of two poems.

The exam: what kind of questions will come up in the exam, how you can get top marks, and what grade 5 and grade 7+ responses look like.

To help you get ready for your exam, each topic includes:

Key quotations to learn
All the poems from the 'Worlds and Lives' anthology are printed in full; useful quotations to memorise are highlighted in pink as these will help you to analyse in the exam and boost your grade.

Additional context to consider
Ideas you can apply to each poem to extend your understanding of how its context has influenced the poet's choices of language, structure and form.

Poetic links
Details of poems with similar themes or features so you know which ones will work well together in the exam.

Sample analysis
An example of the kind of analysis that the examiner will be looking for.

Quick test
A quick-fire test to check you can remember the main points from the topic.

Exam practice
A short writing task so you can practise analysing each poem.

Glossary
Handy lists of literary terms and general words, with easy-to-understand definitions, that you will find useful when revising the 'Worlds and Lives' poetry.

AUTHOR: IAN KIRBY

ebook

To access the ebook version of this Snap Revision Text Guide, visit **collinshub.co.uk/ebooks** and follow the step-by-step instructions.

Published by Collins
An imprint of HarperCollinsPublishers
1 London Bridge Street
London SE1 9GF

HarperCollinsPublishers
Macken House, 39/40 Mayor Street Upper,
Dublin 1, D01 C9W8, Ireland

© HarperCollinsPublishers Limited 2025

ISBN 9780008768935

First published 2025

10 9 8 7 6 5 4 3 2 1

All rights reserved. No part of this publication may be reproduced, stored in a retrieval system, or transmitted, in any form or by any means, electronic, mechanical, photocopying, recording or otherwise, without the prior permission of Collins.

Without limiting the exclusive rights of any author, contributor or the publisher of this publication, any unauthorised use of this publication to train generative artificial intelligence (AI) technologies is expressly prohibited. HarperCollins also exercise their rights under Article 4(3) of the Digital Single Market Directive 2019/790 and expressly reserve this publication from the text and data mining exception.

British Library Cataloguing in Publication Data.

A CIP record of this book is available from the British Library.

Commissioning Editor: Clare Souza
Managing Editor: Shelley Teasdale
Author: Ian Kirby
Typesetting: QBS Learning
Cover designers: Kneath Associates and Sarah Duxbury
Production: Bethany Brohm
Printed in India by Multivista Global Pvt. Ltd.

ACKNOWLEDGEMENTS
The author and publisher are grateful to the copyright holders for permission to use quoted materials and images.

Every effort has been made to trace copyright holders and obtain their permission for the use of copyright material. The author and publisher will gladly receive information enabling them to rectify any error or omission in subsequent editions. All facts are correct at time of going to press.

James Berry, 'On an Afternoon Train from Purley to Victoria, 1955' from *A Story I Am In: Selected Poems* (Bloodaxe Books, 2011); Raman Mundair, 'Name Journeys', *Lovers, Liars, Conjurers and Thieves*, Peepal Tree Press, 2003; 'pot' © shamshad khan; Seni Seneviratne, 'A Wider View', *Wild Cinnamon and Winter Skin*, Peepal Tree Press, 2007; 'Homing' from *Black Country* by Liz Berry published by Chatto & Windus. Copyright © Liz Berry, 2014. Reprinted by permission of The Random House Group Limited; Imtiaz Dharker, 'A century later' from *Over the Moon* (Bloodaxe Books, 2014); 'The Jewellery Maker' © Louisa Adjoa Parker; 'With Birds You're Never Lonely' (37 lines) © Raymond Antrobus 2019, reproduced with kind permission by David Higham Associates; Roger Robinson, 'A Portable Paradise', *A Portable Paradise*, Peepal Tree Press, 2019; Grace Nichols, 'Like an Heiress' from *I Have Crossed an Ocean: Selected Poems* (Bloodaxe Books, 2010); 'Thirteen' from *Poor* by Caleb Femi published by Penguin. Copyright © Caleb Femi, 2020. Reprinted by permission of Penguin Books Limited.

MIX
Paper | Supporting responsible forestry
FSC
www.fsc.org
FSC™ C007454

This book contains FSC™ certified paper and other controlled sources to ensure responsible forest management.

For more information visit: www.harpercollins.co.uk/green

This poem is about...
the peace and harmony in nature, and humankind's failure to follow its example.

How do the first two stanzas establish ideas about the natural and human world?
Throughout the poem, nature is **personified** to emphasise its importance and give it at least equal status to humankind.

The idea of harmony in nature is conveyed through the image of 'a thousand blended notes'; the use of **hyperbole** suggests that this is achieved despite the huge diversity in nature.

As a result of this harmony, the speaker feels a sense of peace and happiness. This is indicated by the **verb 'reclined'** and the **noun phrases** 'sweet mood' and 'pleasant thoughts'.

Wordsworth creates a contrast to this – 'sad thoughts' and 'grieved my heart' – to convey his distress that humankind is not equally harmonious: 'What man has made of man'. He suggests that, unlike in the natural world, people are constantly in conflict and always mistreating each other.

The **metaphor** 'To her fair works did Nature link / The human soul' is used to assert that we are all part of nature, thereby implying that we should know better.

How do stanzas 3–5 develop the idea of harmony in nature?
Wordsworth depicts different elements of nature harmlessly interacting with each other, such as the periwinkle and primrose plants intertwining or the branches catching the breeze. A happy **mood** is further created by describing the birds at play and how each flower 'Enjoys the air it breathes'.

The **noun** 'pleasure' is repeated to convey the joy that this harmony brings to the speaker, implying it could have the same effect on the whole of humankind.

Flowers, trees and birds are described simply: 'green', 'budding', 'hopped and played'. The lack of complexity, and the way that these words link to newness or youthfulness, could suggest the innocence or purity of nature. This is possibly forming a contrast with the sense of conflict and corruption that is created when humankind is being described.

However, the flowers and trees are also personified and the birds are described as having 'thoughts I cannot measure'. Wordsworth could be implying that people don't recognise the importance of nature and what we can learn from it. The idea of immeasurability additionally reminds the reader of nature's eternal life cycle.

How does the final stanza comment on humankind?
The speaker returns to his sadness (or **'lament'**) for humankind.

Nature is presented as having a 'holy plan' and being sent from 'heaven'; by referring back to lines 5–6, it can be inferred that Wordsworth believes the same of humankind.

Lines Written in Early Spring

However, the poem's final image, 'Have I not reason to lament / What man has made of man?' (another reference back to the second **stanza**) suggests that humans are constantly in conflict with each other: we are not following the 'holy plan' and we need to live more harmoniously. Wordsworth frames this image within a **rhetorical question** to indicate that his conclusions about humankind are a fact rather than something to debate.

How does the poem's form contribute to the way meaning is conveyed?

This is a **lyric poem**, a formal type of poetry that expresses personal feelings and emotions.

It is arranged in **quatrains** with an alternate *abab* **rhyme** scheme; the first three lines of each stanza are in **iambic tetrameter**, with a fourth line of **iambic trimeter**.

This regular rhythmic **metre** could help to reinforce the ideas about the harmony of nature and everything being divinely planned.

Additional context to consider

Wordsworth was a Romantic poet. **Romanticism** was an artistic movement that was inspired by nature but was also political and **advocated** social change. The language of the poem clearly relates to these different topics.

Wordsworth's poems can often be linked to the **Industrial Revolution** and its impact on society and nature; he typically idealised **rural** life while criticising **urban** development. This could be linked to the poem's praise of the natural world and the implication that we should be living in closer **alignment** to nature.

At the time the poem was written, Christianity had a large influence on English life and thought. In the final stanza, Wordsworth uses the then dominant belief that God created the world ('If this belief from heaven be sent, / If such be Nature's holy plan') to strengthen his argument that humankind needs to live more harmoniously.

Poetic links

- The natural world in 'Shall earth no more inspire thee', 'With Birds You're Never Lonely', 'A Portable Paradise' and 'Like an Heiress'.
- Connections with places in 'England in 1819', 'Shall earth no more inspire thee', 'In a London Drawingroom', 'On an Afternoon Train…', 'pot', 'A Wider View', 'Homing', 'The Jewellery Maker', 'With Birds You're Never Lonely', 'A Portable Paradise' and 'Like an Heiress'.
- Humankind: conflict, oppression and destruction in 'England in 1819', 'In a London Drawingroom', 'Name Journeys', 'pot', 'Homing', 'A century later', 'Like an Heiress' and 'Thirteen'.

Sample analysis

'Lines Written in Early Spring' and 'In a London Drawingroom' explore different connections between people and places. Wordsworth presents a positive link with a place, conveying how the natural world can bring peace of mind. A calm **atmosphere** is created in 'While in a **grove** I sate reclined, / In that sweet mood' through the use of the **verb phrase** 'sate reclined' to indicate relaxation and inactivity. This is emphasised by the **adjective** 'sweet', suggesting that everything feels perfect and undisturbed. In comparison, Eliot's poem creates a more negative link between people and places. Describing how 'All hurry on & look upon the ground', London is depicted as causing stress and misery. The verb 'hurry' contrasts with Wordsworth's 'reclined', creating a mood of urgency that is highlighted by the way the indefinite **pronoun** 'all' extends it to the city's entire population. The verb phrase 'look upon the ground' adds to this sense of urgency but could also be **symbolic** of unhappiness and hopelessness, suggesting there is nothing positive to see in the city.

Questions

QUICK TEST
1. According to the poem, how is humankind different to nature?
2. How does the speaker feel when thinking about humankind?
3. Why might Wordsworth be using simple images to describe nature?
4. What technique is used in the last two lines of the poem?

EXAM PRACTICE
Using one or two of the highlighted quotations to learn, write a paragraph exploring how Wordsworth feels about nature.

England in 1819
by Percy Bysshe Shelley

An old, mad, blind, despised, and dying King;
Princes, the dregs of their dull race, who flow
Through public scorn,—mud from a muddy spring;
Rulers who neither see nor feel nor know,
5 But leechlike to their fainting country cling
Till they drop, blind in blood, without a blow.
A people starved and stabbed in th' untilled field;
An army, whom liberticide and prey
Makes as a two-edged sword to all who wield;
10 Golden and sanguine laws which tempt and slay;
Religion Christless, Godless—a book sealed;
A senate, Time's worst statute, unrepealed—
Are graves from which a glorious Phantom may
Burst, to illumine our tempestuous day.

This poem is about…
England being a land of **inequality** and **oppression**, ruled by a **corrupt monarchy**.

How do the first three lines criticise the monarchy?
The opening list of adjectives describes the condition of King George III who had been deemed mentally unfit to rule since 1811.

The double meaning of 'blind' accuses the King of lacking social and political awareness. Similarly, 'dying' could also be suggesting what Shelley saw as the overall corrupt **degeneration** of the monarchy.

Additionally, 'despised' asserts that, because of these faults, the King is hated. Shelley's list might be an **allusion** to Shakespeare's famous play *King Lear*: at the start, Lear is presented as an aged **tyrant** with a corrupt family.

Lines 2 and 3 focus their criticism on George IV, the King's son who became the Prince Regent in 1811 and was **notorious** for his extravagant self-indulgence. His love of alcohol is alluded to in the initial metaphor. By comparing him to '**dregs**' (the leftovers from a drink), it suggests that he is worthless and should be thrown away. He is also described as 'dull', implying a lack of intelligence. These two words are **alliterated** to emphasise the line's criticisms.

These two lines also form an **extended metaphor** related to water. The monarchy is described as 'mud from a muddy spring', suggesting that it is morally and biologically corrupt (instead of being pure like normal spring water). This is mocking the effect that centuries of royal **dynasties** intermarrying had on the royal family's gene pool, perhaps implying that this is what made them all 'mad' or 'dull'. The metaphor also accuses the monarchy of being **arrogantly** unconcerned by public **perceptions** ('flow / Through public **scorn**').

How is the criticism of the monarchy developed?
Line 4 uses a **tricolon** – 'neither see nor feel nor know' – to build up the criticism of the monarchy's disregard for normal people. The royal family is depicted as disinterested, lacking in **empathy** and **ignorant**.

Shelley reinforces this through the leech metaphor in lines 5 and 6. The image of blood-sucking and the verb 'cling' suggest the monarchy is taking from the people without giving anything back. The personification – 'fainting country' – indicates that this **exploitation** is harming England.

Shelley asserts that this is all the royal family do until they die: 'drop, blind in blood, without a blow'. The image of blindness suggests they are greedy, focusing on their own gain rather than the needs of the population. The reference to 'without a blow' could imply that no one tries to stop them, perhaps **foreshadowing** the message of the next eight lines.

How does the focus of the poem shift?
In lines 7–9, Shelley responds to the Peterloo Massacre of August 1819: a peaceful political protest was held in St Peter's Field ('th' untilled field') in Manchester but the army charged at the crowd, resulting in eighteen deaths and hundreds of injuries.

England in 1819

The verbs 'starved and stabbed' are alliterated to link why people were asking for political change (inequality had led to poverty and hunger) with the **fate** of those who demanded it; the **plosive** sounds throughout line 7 could also represent violence.

The army is described as a killer of freedom ('liberticide'). The **simile** comparing the army's actions to 'a two-edged sword' could link to the biblical idea that 'all they that take the sword shall perish with the sword', imagining that a **revolution** will avenge the victims.

How is the idea of revolution developed?

Shelley criticises three key aspects of English society: the legal system, the Church and the Government.

The Law is described as 'golden and **sanguine**', using contrasting colours to suggest it misrepresents itself: while it pretends to be looking after the country, it is actually harmful ('sanguine' refers to the colour of blood). This is reinforced through 'tempt and **slay**', again suggesting that it seems like a force for good but can be used to kill.

The Church is depicted as irreligious – 'Christless, Godless'. The phrase 'a book sealed' suggests the Church doesn't believe in freedom and uses the Bible to create **conformity** and a lack of questioning. This is an example of **metonymy** with the 'book' being used to represent the Church of England.

Metaphor is used to describe parliament ('**senate**') as a failed law that should have been abandoned ('Time's worst **statute**, **unrepealed**').

All three institutions are linked to death ('graves') to suggest the harm they cause. However, Shelley uses metaphor to depict how England might eventually revolt: 'a glorious **Phantom** may / Burst, to **illumine** our **tempestuous** day.' The adjective 'tempestuous' summarises the corruption and chaos that Shelley sees in England while 'illumine' uses symbolism of light to suggest hope for a better time. The verb 'burst' could be warning the **establishment** that such a revolution would not be peaceful.

How does the poem's form contribute to the way meaning is conveyed?

The poem is written as a **sonnet**, a form traditionally associated with courtly love; the 'court' referred to the extended household of a royal family. Shelley is deliberately **subverting** the form by using it to criticise the monarchy.

Additional context to consider

Shelley was a Romantic poet. While his work often displayed the movement's typical interest in nature, he was especially political and this is evident from his criticisms of different establishments and of the Peterloo Massacre.

Because the poem was so critical of the royal family and could have led to legal action, it wasn't actually published until after Shelley's death.

Poetic links

- Connections with places in 'Lines Written in Early Spring', 'Shall earth no more inspire thee', 'In a London Drawingroom', 'On an Afternoon Train...', 'pɔt', 'A Wider View', 'Homing', 'The Jewellery Maker', 'With Birds You're Never Lonely', 'A Portable Paradise' and 'Like an Heiress'.
- Connections between people in 'On an Afternoon Train...', 'pɔt', 'A Wider View', 'Homing', 'A century later', 'With Birds You're Never Lonely' and 'A Portable Paradise'.
- Humankind: conflict, oppression and destruction in 'Lines Written in Early Spring', 'In a London Drawingroom', 'Name Journeys', 'pɔt', 'Homing', 'A century later', 'Like an Heiress' and 'Thirteen'.
- Inequality in 'A century later', 'The Jewellery Maker' and 'Thirteen'.

Sample analysis

'England in 1819' and 'Thirteen' criticise the oppressiveness of figures of state authority. Responding to the Peterloo Massacre, Shelley describes 'An army, whom liberticide and prey / Makes as a two-edged sword to all who **wield**' to convey its violent acts of oppression. The nouns 'liberticide and prey' suggest that the army enjoys removing freedom, perhaps seeing people as animals to be hunted. The sword metaphor adds a revolutionary threat to his criticism, imagining this violence will ultimately **rebound** upon the army. Like Shelley, Femi uses metaphor to explore state oppression. The boy's expectation that he is going to be killed – 'You will watch the two men cast lots for your organs' – increases the poem's **tone** of fear, with the single, **end-stopped** line adding to the sense of finality. Similar to 'prey', the noun 'organs' and the verb phrase 'cast lots' make the policemen sound like hunters enjoying themselves. However, the poem doesn't have the revolutionary hope of 'England in 1819', instead using **direct address** and the **modal verb** 'will' to highlight the **inevitability** of **systemic racism** for some communities.

Questions

QUICK TEST
1. How is King George III depicted?
2. What criticisms are made of the monarchy?
3. Which other four establishments are criticised in the poem?
4. What does Shelley imagine happening in England's future?

EXAM PRACTICE
Using one or two of the highlighted quotations to learn, write a paragraph exploring how Shelley criticises the state of the nation in 1819.

England in 1819

Shall earth no more inspire thee
by Emily Brontë

Shall earth no more inspire thee,
Thou lonely dreamer now?
Since passion may not fire thee
Shall Nature cease to bow?

5   Thy mind is ever moving
In regions dark to thee;
Recall its useless roving—
Come back and dwell with me.

I know my mountain breezes
10 Enchant and soothe thee still—
I know my sunshine pleases
Despite thy wayward will.

When day with evening blending
Sinks from the summer sky,
15 I've seen thy spirit bending
In fond idolatry.

I've watched thee every hour;
I know my mighty sway,
I know my magic power
20 To drive thy griefs away.

Few hearts to mortals given
On earth so wildly pine;
Yet none would ask a heaven
More like this earth than thine.

25 Then let my winds caress thee;
Thy comrade let me be—
Since nought beside can bless thee,
Return and dwell with me.

This poem is about…
the positive impact that nature can have on mental health.

How do the first two stanzas establish the addressee's unhappiness?
The opening line (and the title) suggests that the **addressee**'s unhappiness comes from them feeling a lack of inspiration.

This is developed through metaphor: line 3 states that 'passion may not fire thee', suggesting nothing excites or interests the addressee; line 6 refers to their thoughts as 'regions dark to thee', indicating that they are full of misery and confusion, lacking a sense of hope.

The description of the addressee in line 5 as someone whose 'mind is ever moving' implies they are **philosophical**, perhaps a poet. This is also shown in the phrase 'lonely dreamer', with the adjective suggesting that their **temperament** isolates them from others. Although the rhetorical questions in the first stanza are being directed at the addressee, it could be argued that these are the thoughts that are going through their mind.

The addressee appears to have become distanced from the speaker, geographically or emotionally. The speaker's wish to help is conveyed through the opening rhetorical questions as well as the **imperative** 'Recall its useless **roving**', which refers back to line 5 and urges the person to stop thinking so deeply about everything. This is emphasised at the end of the second stanza through another imperative, 'Come back and dwell with me.'

How do stanzas 3–5 suggest the healing power of nature?
The speaker continues to offer comfort through nature – 'I know my sunshine pleases'. The verbs in line 10, 'enchant and soothe', present nature as magical and relaxing.

The repeated use of the **determiner** 'my' indicates that the speaker is nature itself. By personifying nature and giving it a voice, the poet emphasises its power and status (because nature becomes as important as humankind, or more so).

This is continued in lines 18 and 19 – 'I know my mighty sway, / I know my magic power' – where the nouns 'sway' and 'power' suggest an ability to influence thought and feeling. The **repetition** of 'I know' throughout these stanzas implies that nature is all-seeing, like an **omniscient** being, and this is highlighted by the phrase 'I've watched thee'.

Many of these images also refer to the beauty of nature, and a sense of harmony is conveyed through the verb 'blending' in lines 13–14: 'When day with evening blending / Sinks from the summer sky'.

The speaker believes that the addressee still loves nature, and is drawn to it – 'thy spirit bending / In fond **idolatry**'. The speaker promises that, although the addressee is unpredictable and perhaps struggles to control their mood ('thy **wayward** will'), nature can help to 'drive thy griefs away'.

How do the final stanzas summarise the power of nature?

The speaker acknowledges that the addressee is more unhappy than most – 'Few hearts … so wildly pine'. The verb '**pine**' could indicate that someone in their life has died (as could the noun 'griefs' in line 20 and perhaps linking to the reference to 'heaven' in line 23); the **adverb** 'wildly' conveys how deeply this has upset them.

The idea of nature as a healing power continues in its offer of comfort – 'let my winds caress thee' – and friendship, 'Thy **comrade** let me be'. The phrase 'Since nought beside can bless thee' suggests that nature is the only thing that can help. Linking to the verb 'bless', the speaker asserts that the natural world is a place of perfection and, perhaps, holiness: 'Yet none would ask a heaven / More like this earth than thine.'

Many of these images are persuasive. This is emphasised by the repetition of 'let' in lines 25–26 and the final imperative, 'Return and dwell with me.'

How does the poem's form contribute to the way meaning is conveyed?

This is a **dramatic monologue** with the speaker a personification of nature. The use of an unnamed direct addressee could mean the speaker is talking to an individual or humanity as a whole.

The poem's **uniformity** matches the theme of nature being harmonious and bringing peace: the seven quatrains have an *abab* rhyme scheme and the rhythm is iambic. Each stanza's first and third lines have an additional unstressed syllable (a 'feminine ending'), perhaps to mirror the idea of nature soothing the listener.

Additional context to consider

Emily Brontë is linked to both the Romantic movement and the **Victorian** era.

A key **motif** of Romantic poetry was nature as a holy source of inspiration and comfort. The Industrial Revolution and continued urban development of the 18th and 19th centuries meant that there was an increasing separation between nature and everyday life.

This divide would have been apparent to Brontë who lived most of her life in a small industrial town on the edge of the Yorkshire moors. She was brought up in a religious family and her father was an Anglican minister.

Poetic links

- The natural world in 'Lines Written in Early Spring', 'With Birds You're Never Lonely', 'A Portable Paradise' and 'Like an Heiress'.
- Connections with places in 'Lines Written in Early Spring', 'England in 1819', 'In a London Drawingroom', 'On an Afternoon Train…', 'pot', 'A Wider View', 'Homing', 'The Jewellery Maker', 'With Birds You're Never Lonely', 'A Portable Paradise' and 'Like an Heiress'.
- Personal struggles in 'Name Journeys', 'A Wider View', 'Homing', 'With Birds You're Never Lonely' and 'A Portable Paradise'.

Sample analysis

'Shall earth no more inspire thee' and 'Lines Written in Early Spring' present the natural world as a calming place of harmony. Brontë personifies nature as able to 'Enchant and soothe thee still— / … When day with evening blending' and create a calm mood. The verbs 'enchant' and 'soothe' imply nature has a magical ability to lull people into a more relaxed state. This sense of harmony is highlighted by the verb 'blending', suggesting that different aspects of nature do not clash but merge peacefully. Wordsworth opens his poem with a similar depiction, perhaps relating to how both poets are seen as part of the Romantic movement which valued nature as a source of inspiration and joy. The lines 'I heard a thousand blended notes, / While in a grove I sate reclined' also use verbs to create a tranquil mood. Like Brontë, he chooses 'blended' to convey harmony in nature while the phrase 'sate reclined' indicates how it brings relaxation. Linking to Brontë's use of 'soothe', Wordsworth includes different senses to emphasise the calming impact that nature can have on humankind.

Questions

QUICK TEST
1. What appears to be wrong with the person being addressed in the poem?
2. Who or what does the speaker appear to be?
3. What can nature offer the addressee?
4. How does the poem's form reflect the idea that nature is harmonious?

EXAM PRACTICE
Using one or two of the highlighted quotations to learn, write a paragraph exploring how Brontë presents the healing power of nature.

In a London Drawingroom
by George Eliot

The sky is cloudy, yellowed by the smoke.
For view there are the houses opposite
Cutting the sky with one long line of wall
Like solid fog: far as the eye can stretch
5 Monotony of surface & of form
Without a break to hang a guess upon.
No bird can make a shadow as it flies,
For all is shadow, as in ways o'erhung
By thickest canvass, where the golden rays
10 Are clothed in hemp. No figure lingering
Pauses to feed the hunger of the eye
Or rest a little on the lap of life.
All hurry on & look upon the ground,
Or glance unmarking at the passers by
15 The wheels are hurrying too, cabs, carriages
All closed, in multiplied identity.
The world seems one huge prison-house & court
Where men are punished at the slightest cost,
With lowest rate of colour, warmth & joy.

This poem is about…
London being a polluted, busy and oppressive place to live.

How do the first six lines present the city of London?
The image of the sky 'yellowed by the smoke' depicts London as polluted by its industrial factories. The adjective suggests the city looks old and unclean, while the short, single-line sentence emphasises the speaker's disgust at what they see from their window.

An **ironic** tone is added by 'For view there are the houses opposite' because this is not a picturesque 'view'. It also indicates that the speaker thinks the city is overpopulated and overdeveloped. The lack of description suggests they feel everything is the same and lacks individuality or interest.

This idea is developed when the speaker describes the houses – 'far as the eye can stretch / Monotony of surface & of form' – with the noun '**monotony**' indicating sameness and suggesting they are boring to look at. Linking such uniformity to 'surface' and 'form' highlights how the city lacks character, appearing unnaturally similar and faceless. There is perhaps some hyperbole in the phrase 'far as the eye can stretch', creating the impression that the houses go on forever, without changing.

The speaker emphasises this by describing how they continue 'Without a break', suggesting their ugliness is unrelenting and perhaps almost exhausting to look at. The old-fashioned, **colloquial** phrase 'hang a guess upon' asserts that there is nothing different or intriguing about any of the houses.

The simile 'one long line of wall / Like solid fog' also depicts dull sameness with the **consonance** of 'l' perhaps mirroring the idea of repetitiveness. The comparison to fog implies the houses create an oppressive atmosphere, as if the speaker feels surrounded. The adjective 'solid' adds to this by suggesting impenetrability, indicating that the speaker feels they cannot escape.

The violent verb phrase 'cutting the sky' suggests that urban development is attacking nature: it is not just blocking the view but metaphorically causing it physical harm.

How do lines 7–10 develop the conflict between nature and urbanisation?
Eliot uses darkness to suggest the impact of overdevelopment and to symbolise people's unhappiness. The simile 'as in ways o'erhung / By thickest canvass' suggests that any natural light to the street is being blocked.

This is emphasised by the metaphor 'golden rays / Are clothed in **hemp**', as if a sack has been thrown over the city. The adjective 'golden' symbolises the importance and beauty of nature, forming a contrast with the repetition of the noun 'shadow'.

By noting that 'No bird can make a shadow as it flies', the poem also suggests that the city seems abnormal, defying the laws of nature.

How does the second half of the poem present the people of London?

The phrase 'No figure lingering / Pauses to feed the hunger of the eye' uses metaphor to suggest that – because everything looks the same – the people are discontented or even lifeless. Their **despondency** is emphasised by the description of how they just 'look upon the ground'.

This unhappiness is related to being constantly busy (no one is 'lingering' or 'pauses'). An atmosphere of urgency and stress is built up by the verb phrase 'All hurry on' and the comment that people do not 'rest a little on the lap of life'. The noun 'lap' could be personification, suggesting people should stop and allow themselves to be comforted by the good things in life; alternatively, it may be metaphor, depicting life as a constant, competitive race.

Eliot links this to the city's lack of individuality, adding that people 'glance unmarking at the passers by' to imply that no one knows, or cares about, anyone else. The hectic traffic is presented as endless and lacking any uniqueness – 'The wheels are hurrying too, cabs, carriages / All closed, in multiplied identity'. The personification could imply that there is no difference between the people and the traffic: both are lifeless, busy machines.

The last three lines summarise London's problems. Metaphor presents it as a place that lacks freedom and identity – 'one huge prison-house' – in which people are constantly judging one another, 'court'. It is without happiness or feeling, 'lowest rate of colour, warmth & joy', with the **superlative** and the tricolon emphasising what is missing. The reference to how 'men are punished at the slightest cost' might also criticise England's lack of social care and how easy it was for people to find themselves struggling financially and then facing the **workhouse**. Describing London as the 'world' might imply that the people cannot imagine, or have no way of making, a life beyond the city and are therefore trapped.

How does the poem's form contribute to the way meaning is conveyed?

The poem is not broken into stanzas and it contains much **enjambment**. This creates a mood of relentlessness as the poem is always moving forward, without pause, matching the depiction of London life.

The **iambic pentameter** creates a regular rhythm that could be mirroring the images of constant routine and lack of freedom.

> ### Additional context to consider
>
> George Eliot moved to London in 1850 and wrote this poem in 1865. By this time, the Industrial Revolution had transformed London into an overcrowded and overdeveloped city that suffered from many social problems, such as poverty and disease.
>
> Writers of the Victorian period often focused on **social realism** and the importance of place.
>
> The poet removes herself from the text, using the **third person** rather than the **first person**. This makes the poem less about her own experience and more about the lives of everyone in London. The present tense creates greater immediacy, highlighting that the poem isn't a reflection on some past experience but – writing in 1865 – what life is like now.

Poetic links

- The urban world and pollution in 'A Wider View' and 'Like an Heiress'.
- Connections with places in 'Lines Written in Early Spring', 'England in 1819', 'Shall earth no more inspire thee', 'On an Afternoon Train…', 'pot', 'A Wider View', 'Homing', 'The Jewellery Maker', 'With Birds You're Never Lonely', 'A Portable Paradise' and 'Like an Heiress'.
- Humankind: conflict, oppression and destruction in 'Lines Written in Early Spring', 'England in 1819', 'Name Journeys', 'pot', 'Homing', 'A century later', 'Like an Heiress' and 'Thirteen'.

Sample analysis

Despite being written a century apart, 'In a London Drawingroom' and 'Like an Heiress' both criticise the pollution of our world. Eliot describes how the sky of Victorian London is 'cloudy, yellowed by the smoke' of the industrialised factories that filled the city. The adjective 'yellowed' suggests uncleanliness and presents the speaker as disgusted by what they can see. Referring to the clouds, Eliot implies that the smoke is damaging the natural world and that this pollution is spreading everywhere. Similarly, Nichols depicts a 'wave of rubbish against the old seawall – / used car tyres, plastic bottles, styrofoam cups', using more modern images to convey present-day pollution in Guyana. The metaphor implies that the sea has become permanently polluted, making water and rubbish the same matter. This is emphasised by how the tricolon builds up the different sources of the pollution.

Questions

QUICK TEST
1. What is the immediate view that the speaker sees from their front window?
2. What are the houses of London compared to?
3. What do the people of London appear to feel about their lives?
4. Is life in London depicted as relaxed or stressful?

EXAM PRACTICE
Using one or two of the highlighted quotations to learn, write a paragraph exploring how Eliot presents London as an unpleasant city.

On an Afternoon Train from Purley to Victoria, 1955 by James Berry

Hello, she said, and startled me.
Nice day. Nice day I agreed.
I am a Quaker she said and Sunday
I was moved in silence
5   to speak a poem loudly
for racial brotherhood.

I was thoughtful, then said
what poem came on like that?
One the moment inspired she said.
10 I was again thoughtful.

Inexplicably I saw
empty city streets lit dimly
in a day's first hours.
Alongside in darkness
15 was my father's big banana field.

Where are you from? she said.
Jamaica I said.
What part of Africa is Jamaica? she said.
Where Ireland is near Lapland I said.
20 Hard to see why you leave
such sunny country she said.
Snow falls elsewhere I said.
So sincere she was beautiful
as people sat down around us.

This poem is about...
a chance meeting, and reflections on race and belonging.

How does the title and first stanza establish the chance meeting?
The title of the poem suggests a normal, unremarkable setting: an afternoon, on an unspecified day in 1955, travelling by train between two areas of London.

However, the poem opens abruptly with a single word of speech, 'Hello'. There is a tone of surprise in the verb phrase 'startled me', indicating that the speaker of the poem is unused to strangers being friendly, perhaps due to him being of a different race to most Londoners at the time.

When the person adds 'Nice day', it is simply repeated by the speaker. This, along with the short sentence chosen by the poet, emphasises that he is not used to such a situation.

The woman is presented differently to the speaker: she is the **instigator** of the conversation, being more open and giving personal information. As well as revealing her religion ('Quaker'), she shares the **profound** experience of being 'moved in silence / to speak'. This refers to a key part of the Quaker faith: in communal worship, they wait in silence until they feel the spirit has prompted them to contribute. The similarity between the situation of worship and the situation on the train (speaking aloud when no one is talking) could suggest that her faith has encouraged her to talk to this stranger.

Across her four lines of speech, the enjambment creates a lack of hesitancy which could make the woman seem more genuine. The speaker later highlights this in line 23 – 'So sincere she was beautiful'.

A connection between the woman and the speaker is established through the references to 'racial **brotherhood**' and poetry. The woman's **dialogue** also includes some **non-standard English** (such as line 3 lacking the **preposition** 'on') which could suggest that, like the speaker, she is an immigrant.

How do the second and third stanzas convey the effect of this meeting on the speaker?
The speaker's changing attitude towards the woman is shown in his friendlier tone, engaging with their conversation by asking a question.

Their increasing connection is suggested by the repetition of him being 'thoughtful' about what she is saying. The adjective 'thoughtful' also connects to her reference to herself as being 'inspired' as both words relate to ideas entering the mind.

This connection is developed when the speaker has a sudden vision, like the woman's inspiration at her Quaker meeting. The image of city streets at dawn ('in a day's first hours') could symbolise his isolation as an immigrant, with the adjective 'empty' and the adverb 'dimly' suggesting loneliness and unhappiness. **Simultaneously**, he sees his 'father's big banana field' which might indicate homesickness. The **juxtaposition** ('Alongside') of urban and rural images also conveys how different the speaker finds life in London. However, the field being depicted in 'darkness' may imply that home wasn't perfect.

On an Afternoon Train from Purley to Victoria, 1955

How does the poet further explore connection and disconnection?

The connection between the speaker and the woman continues when she asks 'Where are you from?', as if reading the thoughts he had in the previous stanza. However, she possibly displays unintentional racism in asking the question and this is heightened when she presumes Jamaica is part of Africa, causing him to joke 'Where Ireland is near Lapland'.

The poet develops this combination of connection and disconnection through different perceptions of Jamaica. While the woman displays **idealism** ('such sunny country') and cannot understand him wanting to come to London ('Hard to see why you leave'), the speaker suggests Jamaica doesn't have everything ('Snow falls elsewhere'). The contrasting imagery could convey that nowhere is perfect: wherever you go, life is simply different rather than better.

The speaker appears to forgive the woman's uninformed speech ('So sincere she was beautiful') and refers to them both as 'us'. This pronoun connects them while also appearing to separate them from the other travellers – 'people sat down around us'.

How does the poem's form contribute to the way meaning is conveyed?

The poem is written in **free verse**, with the lack of rhyme and metre matching its conversational style; similarly, most of the language is **prosaic** rather than metaphorical.

Each stanza presents a different aspect of the conversation between the woman and the speaker.

Additional context to consider

James Berry was born in Jamaica and moved to London in the 1940s. He was part of the 'Windrush generation' of people who left the Caribbean for Britain after the Second World War. Mixing English and Jamaican **patois**, Berry often wrote about the triumphs and tensions of immigration.

It is estimated that at the start of the 1950s, only about 20,000 people in Britain were non-White; this was less than 0.04% of the population.

The poem appears to be **autobiographical**. Writing in the first person, and partly making use of a **duologue**, adds greater intimacy. It is presented as a brief, random moment but one that is representative of different attitudes the speaker has experienced.

The poem also refers to Quakers – a religious group that has a strong belief in equality.

Poetic links

- Connections with places in 'Lines Written in Early Spring', 'England in 1819', 'Shall earth no more inspire thee', 'In a London Drawingroom', 'pot', 'A Wider View', 'Homing', 'The Jewellery Maker', 'With Birds You're Never Lonely', 'A Portable Paradise' and 'Like an Heiress'.
- Connections between people in 'England in 1819', 'pot', 'A Wider View', 'Homing', 'A century later', 'With Birds You're Never Lonely' and 'A Portable Paradise'.
- Heritage and identity in 'Name Journeys', 'pot', 'A Wider View', 'Homing', 'The Jewellery Maker', 'With Birds You're Never Lonely', 'A Portable Paradise', 'Like an Heiress' and 'Thirteen'.

Sample analysis

'On an Afternoon Train...' and 'With Birds You're Never Lonely' present different ideas about being alone. Although the speaker in Berry's poem appears to live in the busy capital city, it suggests he feels lonely. Perhaps linking to being from a racial minority in the 1950s, his image of 'empty city streets lit dimly' could symbolise isolation. This is highlighted by the adjective 'empty' while the adverb 'dimly' may also convey unhappiness or hopelessness. In comparison, Antrobus's speaker describes an experience of 'silence that was not an absence' while in an isolated Zelandia forest. Although the two nouns used have a similar meaning, the verb phrase 'was not' distinguishes between them to emphasise that the speaker feels a sense of solitude in nature. This is despite, or perhaps because of, there being no other people around which contrasts with Berry's urban loneliness.

Questions

QUICK TEST
1. How does the speaker react when the woman first talks to him?
2. How does their interaction seem initially awkward?
3. What two-part vision does the speaker have while talking to the woman?
4. In what way might the woman be displaying unintentional racism?

EXAM PRACTICE
Using one or two of the highlighted quotations to learn, write a paragraph exploring how Berry presents connections between people or places.

Name Journeys by Raman Mundair

Like Rama I have felt the wilderness
but I have not been blessed

with a companion as sweet as she,
Sita; loyal, pure and true of heart.

5 Like her I have been chastened
through trial by fire. Sita and I,

spiritual sari-sisters entwined
in an infinite silk that would swathe

Draupadi's blush. My name
10 a journey between rough and smooth,

an interlacing of banyan leaves with sugar
cane. Woven tapestries of journeys;

travelling from South
to North, where the Punjabi in my mouth

15 became dislodged as milk teeth fell
and hit infertile English soil.

My mouth toiled to accommodate
the rough musicality of Mancunian vowels

and my name became a stumble
20 that filled English mouths

with a discordant rhyme, an exotic
rhythm dulled, my voice a mystery

in the Anglo echo chamber –
void of history and memory.

This poem is about…

the importance of **heritage** and the challenges of being an immigrant.

How do the opening five stanzas use Hinduism to explore identity?

The first five **couplets** describe the poet's life through references to three figures in Hinduism: the major **deities** of Rama and Sita, who were married, and the empress Draupadi.

Mundair asserts the importance of Hinduism to her identity by using a metaphor to join herself with Sita: 'spiritual sari-sisters entwined / in an infinite silk'. The word 'entwined' indicates that she cannot be separated from her heritage and this is emphasised by the use of **sibilance** to link the words in the metaphor together. The adjective 'infinite' suggests this connection will last forever.

The poet compares herself to Rama, who faced many challenges ('felt the **wilderness**'), indicating that she has had a difficult life. This is emphasised by also comparing herself to Sita in the metaphor '**chastened** / through trial by fire', conveying how she has felt harshly judged and punished. Lines 8–9 return to this by referencing Draupadi's 'blush' (relating to a story in which men try to strip the Empress naked) to imply she has been made to feel uncomfortable by sexist attitudes in society. Using her sari to symbolise her faith, the verb '**swathe**' could suggest that her beliefs have helped to protect her

She adds that, unlike Rama who married Sita, she has 'not been blessed' with a partner. This verb phrase indicates the speaker feels unfortunate at not having someone in her life. The adjectives that describe Sita ('sweet' and the tricolon, 'loyal, pure and true') build up a tone of sadness because they highlight different qualities that she has perhaps needed from others but not found.

How do stanzas 5–8 explore immigration?

In stanza five, the poet changes her focus to how she moved from India to England as a child. The significance of this to her identity and life story is conveyed through the metaphors 'My name / a journey' and 'Woven tapestries of journeys'.

The reference to contrasting textures – 'rough and smooth' – implies that immigration was a mix of bad times and good times, or challenges and pleasures. This is emphasised through a similar contrast of softness ('banyan leaves') and hardness ('sugar cane').

A particular challenge was the need to learn a new language. Her **Punjabi** is described as becoming 'dislodged' and landing on '**infertile** English soil'. These metaphors suggest that she felt disconnected from her heritage and that it was not valued or encouraged in England. The reference to 'milk teeth' adds to the distressing tone by emphasising how young she was at the time.

How do the final stanzas present the challenges of living in a different country?

The last four couplets further explore the idea of having to adopt a new language.

She praises the Mancunian accent for its 'rough musicality' but the metaphor 'my mouth toiled to accommodate' explains how she struggled to form its different sounds. The verb 'toiled' indicates that she tried hard, perhaps seeing it as a way to fit in.

Similarly, she uses metaphor to convey how the people she met struggled to pronounce her name: 'a stumble / that filled English mouths'. The noun 'stumble' could indicate their embarrassment; it might also suggest this became an obstacle for her when meeting people or how it made her feel like a problem. This is emphasised by the noun phrase '**discordant** rhyme', suggesting it made her feel out of place in English culture.

The tone of frustration shifts to sadness as she describes the pronunciation of her name as an 'exotic / rhythm dulled'. The verb 'dulled' suggests her name was made to sound more English, perhaps implying that she then felt the need to present herself this way. Her heritage wasn't seen by others as exciting or fascinating ('exotic') so she **suppressed** it.

The poet describes her own voice as 'a mystery / in the Anglo echo chamber'. This metaphor suggests that she lost touch with her sense of self ('mystery') because, when she spoke English, only a small remnant of her heritage remained ('echo'). She emphasises this by depicting her speech as 'void of history and memory', indicating that it didn't reflect her cultural identity.

How does the poem's form contribute to the way meaning is conveyed?

The poem is a variation on a **ghazal**, a form of Indian poetry that often explores spiritual love or the pain of loss or separation. This matches the poem's themes of immigration and heritage.

A ghazal is usually organised into individual couplets with a set rhythm. However, the poet's use of free verse and enjambment are perhaps subtly criticising how she was made to feel the need to fit in as a child.

Additional context to consider

Mundair was born in India and moved to the UK when she was a child; this experience informs the whole poem.

She is disabled, **neuro-diverse** and identifies as **Queer**. The poem's images and ideas often contrast with traditional expectations or structures such as **patriarchy**, dominant White culture and **heteronormativity**.

Writing in the first person adds greater intimacy to the poem. The inclusion of words linked to Indian culture relates to the speaker's **dual heritage**.

Poetic links

- Heritage and identity in 'On an Afternoon Train...', 'pot', 'A Wider View', 'Homing', 'The Jewellery Maker', 'With Birds You're Never Lonely', 'A Portable Paradise', 'Like an Heiress' and 'Thirteen'.
- Immigration in 'A Wider View' and 'A Portable Paradise'.
- Humankind: conflict, oppression and destruction in 'Lines Written in Early Spring', 'England in 1819', 'In a London Drawingroom', 'pot', 'Homing', 'A century later', 'Like an Heiress' and 'Thirteen'.
- Personal struggles in 'Shall earth no more inspire thee', 'A Wider View', 'Homing', 'With Birds You're Never Lonely' and 'A Portable Paradise'.

Sample analysis

'Name Journeys' and 'A Wider View' explore the different challenges of immigrating to England. Mundair uses a metaphor to present her personal experience of struggling to fit in due to having a different cultural identity. Recalling how her 'mouth toiled to accommodate' the sounds of a new language, the verbs 'toiled' and 'accommodate' indicate that she worked hard to seem like everyone else but speaking English always felt unnatural. In comparison, Seneviratne imagines the life of her great-great-grandfather. By describing his 'eyes dry with dust / from twelve hours combing flax', she focuses more on the physical and economic challenges of immigration. The adjective phrase 'dry with dust' evokes discomfort and tiredness, emphasised by the reference to working for 'twelve hours'. His job is presented as manual labour, suggesting it was difficult and low paid, reflecting how he strove to improve his family's new life.

Questions

QUICK TEST
1. Which three figures of Hinduism are referenced in the poem?
2. In what ways does the poet feel similar to these religious figures?
3. What challenge did she encounter when living in England?
4. What did other people find challenging when they met her?

EXAM PRACTICE
Using one or two of the highlighted quotations to learn, write a paragraph exploring how Mundair presents the loss of cultural identity.

pot by Shamshad Khan

so big - they said you shouldn't really be moved

so fragile you might break

you could be from anywhere pot

styles have travelled just like terracotta
5 you could almost be an english pot

but I know you're not.

I know half of the story pot
of where you come from
of how you got here

10 but I need you to tell me the rest pot

tell me

did they say you were bought pot
a looter's deal done
the whole lot
15 sold to the gentleman in the grey hat

or
did they say you were lost pot
finders are keepers you know pot

or
20   did they say they didn't notice you pot
     must have slipped onto the white sailing yacht

     bound for england.

     someone
     somewhere

25   will have missed you pot
     gone out looking for you pot
     because
     someone
     somewhere

30   made you
     fingernails
     pressed
     snake patterned you pot
     washed you pot
35   used you pot
     loved you pot

         if I could shatter this glass
         I would take you back myself pot.

     you think they wouldn't recognise you pot

40   say diaspora
     you left now
     you're not really one of us.

pot I've been back to where my family's from
　　　they were happy
45　to see me
　　　laughed a lot
　　　said I was more asian than the asians pot
　　　I was pot

　　　imagine.
50　the hot sun on your back

　　　feel flies settle on your skin
　　　warm grain poured inside

　　　empty pot
　　　growl if you hear me

55　pot?

　　　pot?

Dedicated to a Nigerian pot currently incarcerated in the Manchester Museum without charge or access to legal representation.

This poem is about...

cultural **repatriation**, **colonialism** and migration; the museum pot represents how other cultures have been treated and perceived by White Europeans.

How do lines 1–9 introduce the issue of stolen cultural artefacts?

The poem begins by addressing the pot, indicating the significance of this seemingly unimportant, everyday object.

The adjectives and repeated **intensifier** 'so big ... so fragile' present the pot as an old and impressive **artefact** that needs to be looked after. However, it is implied that these are also the excuses used by museum directors for not returning stolen artefacts: 'they said you shouldn't really be moved ... you might break'. The modal verbs suggest the possibility of damage but are also indefinite, indicating that it could be safe to return it to its country of origin.

Lines 7–9 start to explore the idea of "whitewashed" historical narratives about colonialism, where negative aspects of history are covered up so the person telling that history does not look bad. The speaker says they only know 'half of the story' of how the pot reached England – in other words, an official story that doesn't admit the artefact was stolen.

How do lines 10–38 explore the issue of cultural colonialism?

The importance of historical truth, and how it shapes our modern identities, is conveyed by the speaker's 'need' to know what happened to the artefact. The pot's individual story represents the wider history of colonialism and its impact on people.

The speaker wants to hear the real story from the pot ('you'), rather than the museum's version, and this is emphasised by the repetition of the verb phrase 'tell me' in its own two-word stanza.

Lines 12–22 present different **euphemistic** stories of the pot's theft. The anaphora 'or / did they say' introduces a series of rhetorical questions that have an increasingly disbelieving tone. The juxtaposition of 'bought' and 'looter' highlights the difference between the official story and the truth, while the use of the colloquialism 'finders are keepers' implies that people don't take this issue seriously enough. The stories have a decreasing involvement of people and become increasingly unlikely: the pot might have been 'lost' or may have impossibly smuggled *itself* on board ('they didn't notice you pot / must have slipped onto'). This suggests that people linked to colonialism are claiming innocence while hiding the truth. However, the 'white' boat going to 'england' indicates that this was cultural theft.

Images of loss – 'missed you ... gone out looking for you' – convey the significance of cultural artefacts to their country of origin. This significance is emphasised by the list of verbs in lines 30–36 ('made', 'pressed', 'washed', 'used', 'loved'), linking to the creation of the pot. The speaker wishes to return the pot, an act of cultural repatriation. The verb 'shatter' imagines breaking the display glass while also indicating the poet's sense of outrage towards colonialism. Modal verbs ('could', 'would') imply the speaker's feeling of helplessness at not being able to resolve the issue.

How is the pot used to explore cultural identity?

The pot could be interpreted as representing people whose families immigrated to Britain from different parts of its old **empire**. In lines 5–6, the pot is described as 'almost' English before the speaker adds 'but I know you're not', perhaps conveying how people with dual heritages sometimes feel that they don't fit in with British society.

To explore people's relationships with their heritage, the poet imagines the pot returning home. In line 40, the noun **'diaspora'** (the spread of people from their homeland) is linked to the fear of losing one's cultural identity: 'you're not really one of us'.

pot

However, the speaker's experience of returning 'to where my family's from' and being welcomed ('they were happy / to see me / laughed a lot') provides reassurance. This is heightened by the humorous tone when relating being told, 'I was more asian than the asians'.

The speaker uses the senses to encourage the pot to return home – 'imagine. / the hot sun on your back', suggesting it will make the pot feel whole again: 'warm grain poured inside / empty pot'. The pot's current emptiness, and perhaps anger, are suggested in the line 'growl if you hear me'.

The last two stanzas feature a repeated one-word question – 'pot? / pot?' – to emphasise the importance of the artefact's viewpoint (rather than that of the museum). The pauses that are created encourage the reader to think about the **ethical** questions being raised.

How does the poem's form contribute to the way meaning is conveyed?

The poet writes in free verse and does not use a clear stanza structure, perhaps to reflect the ideas of displacement and lost connections. Short lines, single-line stanzas and anaphora are regularly used to emphasise ideas, thereby creating a more persuasive argument.

Additional context to consider

Shamshad Khan is a second-generation British Asian from Manchester. The poem appears to be autobiographical and writing in the first person makes it more personal.

By avoiding standard grammar, the poet could be rejecting traditional expectations; this mirrors her rejection of official attitudes to stolen cultural artefacts.

Museums across Britain contain thousands of contested artefacts that people believe should be returned to their native countries, including human remains.

The dedication at the end of the poem also links the pot to prisoners who have been imprisoned 'without charge or access to legal representation', as was happening at Guantanamo Bay when the poem was published in 2007.

Poetic links

- Connections with places in 'Lines Written in Early Spring', 'England in 1819', 'Shall earth no more inspire thee', 'In a London Drawingroom', 'On an Afternoon Train…', 'A Wider View', 'Homing', 'The Jewellery Maker', 'With Birds You're Never Lonely', 'A Portable Paradise' and 'Like an Heiress'.
- Connections between people in 'England in 1819', 'On an Afternoon Train…', 'A Wider View', 'Homing', 'A century later', 'With Birds You're Never Lonely' and 'A Portable Paradise'.
- Heritage and identity in 'On an Afternoon Train…', 'Name Journeys', 'A Wider View', 'Homing', 'The Jewellery Maker', 'With Birds You're Never Lonely', 'A Portable Paradise', 'Like an Heiress' and 'Thirteen'.
- Humankind: conflict, oppression and destruction in 'Lines Written in Early Spring', 'England in 1819', 'In a London Drawingroom', 'Name Journeys', 'Homing', 'A century later', 'Like an Heiress' and 'Thirteen'.

Sample analysis

The poems 'pot' and 'England in 1819' present a desire for change. Khan explores the modern issue of cultural repatriation, relating to the number of contested artefacts in British museums. The speaker's pledge – 'if I could shatter this glass / I would take you back myself' – uses the verb phrase 'take you back myself' to convey their commitment to the issue. However, the modal verbs 'could' and 'would' allude to how larger, political structures form an **insurmountable** obstacle to change. While the verb 'shatter' suggests the speaker's willingness to act, it could also indicate their anger at feeling unable to succeed. Shelley also presents desire for change through his wish for a social revolution to overthrow what he saw as England's corrupt establishment. His metaphor 'a glorious Phantom may / Burst, to illumine our tempestuous day' depicts all the victims of the state rising up to create a better future. The adjective 'glorious' and the verb 'illumine' indicate how this change would improve England; the reference to light symbolises truth and purity, contrasting with the idea of corruption and chaos that is suggested by the adjective 'tempestuous'. Like Khan, Shelley combines a violent verb ('burst') with a modal verb ('may') but his tone is much more hopeful, asserting his belief that change is possible.

Questions

QUICK TEST
1. Who or what is the poem addressed to?
2. What does the speaker want to know about the pot?
3. What does the speaker want to do with the pot?
4. What different things can the pot represent?

EXAM PRACTICE
Using one or two of the highlighted quotations to learn, write a paragraph exploring how Khan presents some of the challenges faced by people with a dual heritage.

A Wider View by Seni Seneviratne

From the backyard of his back-to-back,
my great-great-grandad searched for spaces
in the smoke-filled sky to stack his dreams,
high enough above the cholera to keep them
5   and his newborn safe from harm.

In eighteen sixty-nine, eyes dry with dust
from twelve hours combing flax beneath
the conicals of light in Marshall's Temple Mill,
he took the long way home because
10   he craved the comfort of a wider view.

As he passed the panelled gates of Tower Works,
the tall octagonal crown of Harding's chimney
drew his sights beyond the limits of his working life
drowned the din of engines, looms and shuttles
15   with imagined peals of ringing bells.

Today, my footsteps echo in the sodium gloom
of Neville Street's Dark Arches and the red-brick vaults
begin to moan as time, collapsing in the River Aire,
sweeps me out to meet him on the Wharf.

20   We stand now, timeless in the flux of time, anchored
only by the axis of our gaze – a ventilation shaft
with gilded tiles, and Giotto's geometric lines –
while the curve of past and future generations
arcs between us.

This poem is about…

links between the past and present; the poet describes her great-great-grandfather's experience of living in Leeds in 1869, alongside her own life in the modern-day city.

How does the first stanza present 19th-century Leeds?

The poet presents the city as cramped by referring to her great-great-grandfather's 'back-to-back', a type of terraced housing that immediately adjoined, or was built very close to, the rear of the property behind it. This is emphasised by describing how he 'searched for spaces', with the verb indicating it was difficult to find anywhere open and airy.

The sense of gloom and oppression is built up by the reference to the 'smoke-filled sky', depicting the pollution from the industrialised factories. Additionally, the city is presented as dangerously unhygienic with the reference to '**cholera**', a disease linked to unclean water and inadequate sewage disposal. This relates back to 'searched for spaces' in line 2, conveying her great-great-grandfather's desperation to find somewhere clean to keep 'his newborn safe from harm'.

Leeds appears to lack hope. The metaphor 'stack his dreams' conveys her great-great-grandfather's wish to build a good life in Britain. However, the problems described in the stanza are a barrier to this, creating an increasing tone of **disillusionment**.

How do stanzas 2 and 3 explore her great-great-grandfather's life in 1869?

The great-great-grandfather is depicted as working hard at the Temple Mill factory and different senses are incorporated to convey his experience. Describing his 'eyes dry with dust / from twelve hours combing flax' highlights how tiring this manual labour would have been while the physical discomfort is emphasised by alliterating 'dry' and 'dust'.

An overwhelming noise is presented through the unpleasant noun 'din'; this is built up by the tricolon 'engines, looms and shuttles', detailing the different parts of the loud machinery. The '**conicals** of light' indicate the factory's gloominess, suggesting he felt trapped but also possibly symbolising glimpses of hope. Furthermore, the reference to 'the limits of his working life' implies he didn't get time for anything else.

His dispiriting work is highlighted by how much he 'craved the comfort of a wider view'. The noun 'comfort' suggests he needed some relief and this is emphasised by the desperation within the verb 'craved'. The phrase 'wider view' returns to the motif of wanting space but could also represent the idea of him seeing beyond the moment to the better future he is trying to build for his family.

This is also conveyed through metaphor when the mill's loudness is 'drowned' out by the unusually beautiful Italian-style architecture of the Tower Works factory. The tower appears to symbolise what can be achieved and built in life, with the **regal** imagery of its 'tall octagonal crown' indicating his respect for hard work as well as the more comfortable life he hoped to attain. The 'crown' could even symbolise Britain and its monarchy being the heart of the Empire; the perception of it as a place of riches may have been one of his reasons for immigrating. The subsequent image of 'imagined peals of ringing bells' implies happiness, celebration and perhaps renewed **resilience**.

A Wider View

How do the last two stanzas link the past with the present?

The last two stanzas focus on Leeds 'today'. A link in time is created by the speaker walking beneath the historic 'Dark Arches', an engineering achievement completed in 1869 to support a railway. Time is also symbolised by how her footsteps create an 'echo'.

The poet creates a strange image of past and present merging as she is brought together with her great-great-grandfather. A dramatic atmosphere is built up by the personification ('red-brick vaults / begin to moan') and metaphor ('as time, collapsing ... / sweeps me out to meet him') that depict this impossible event.

The architecture of Tower Works is once more described – 'gilded tiles, and Giotto's geometric lines'. She describes this historical landmark as the 'axis of our gaze', because she is looking at it now just as her great-great-grandfather did in 1869. The poet appears to be theorising that all time exists simultaneously and this is developed through the metaphor 'the curve of past and future generations / arcs between us' to assert the importance of heritage to one's identity. This could link back to the title, suggesting that we are more than just our immediate, narrow existence.

How does the poem's form contribute to the way meaning is conveyed?

The idea that time merges and our present is related to our past may be reflected in the poem's form and structure. Although the stanzas clearly separate the narratives of then and now, free verse and enjambment reduce any sense of a fixed structure. Additionally, the alliteration throughout the poem could be to emphasise the motif of links and patterns.

Additional context to consider

Seneviratne was born and raised in Leeds; her great-great-grandfather immigrated from Sri Lanka in the 1800s. Although she is imagining what his life would have been like and uses elements of fantasy towards the end of the poem, she uses various **proper nouns** to create a realistic sense of place.

The Industrial Revolution led to Leeds becoming one of the country's key factory towns. This brought with it many problems typical of urban growth: overpopulation, poor housing and hygiene, disease and poverty.

The combination of first and third person, and of past and present tense, links to how the poem explores connections between people and the impact of this on their identities.

Poetic links

- The urban world and pollution in 'In a London Drawingroom' and 'Like an Heiress'.
- Connections with places in 'Lines Written in Early Spring', 'England in 1819', 'Shall earth no more inspire thee', 'In a London Drawingroom', 'On an Afternoon Train...', 'pot', 'Homing', 'The Jewellery Maker', 'With Birds You're Never Lonely', 'A Portable Paradise' and 'Like an Heiress'.
- Connections between people in 'England in 1819', 'On an Afternoon Train...', 'pot', 'Homing', 'A century later', 'With Birds You're Never Lonely' and 'A Portable Paradise'.
- Heritage and identity in 'On an Afternoon Train...', 'Name Journeys', 'pot', 'Homing', 'The Jewellery Maker', 'With Birds You're Never Lonely', 'A Portable Paradise', 'Like an Heiress' and 'Thirteen'.
- Immigration in 'Name Journeys' and 'A Portable Paradise'.
- Personal struggles in 'Shall earth no more inspire thee', 'Name Journeys', 'Homing', 'With Birds You're Never Lonely' and 'A Portable Paradise'.
- Hopes and fears in 'A century later', 'The Jewellery Maker', 'A Portable Paradise' and 'Thirteen'.

Sample analysis

'A Wider View' and 'pot' both use metaphor to explore the importance of heritage. Seneviratne describes how 'the curve of past and future generations / arcs between us' to draw a link between herself and her great-great-grandfather. While the noun 'curve' establishes the idea of a connection, the verb 'arcs' implies that it forms a circle: understanding her family's past is important to her, just as hopes for his family's future were important for him. Khan makes similar use of metaphor – 'warm grain poured inside / empty pot' – to represent the importance of heritage. Images of emptiness and fullness are juxtaposed to suggest the impact of understanding one's origins, with the adjective 'warm' implying the comfort that comes from this knowledge. As a pot is made to contain something, the poet is also using the image of 'grain poured inside' to assert that one's heritage is life-affirming and creates a sense of wholeness or fulfilment.

Questions

QUICK TEST
1. Where and when are the first three stanzas of the poem set?
2. What kind of life did the speaker's great-great-grandfather have?
3. What building is used to link the speaker and her great-great-grandfather?
4. What is the poet's message about our past and present?

EXAM PRACTICE
Using one or two of the highlighted quotations to learn, write a paragraph exploring how Seneviratne presents struggle and hardship.

Homing by Liz Berry

For years you kept your accent
in a box beneath the bed,
the lock rusted shut by hours of elocution
how now brown cow
5   the teacher's ruler across your legs.

We heard it escape sometimes,
a guttural *uh* on the phone to your sister,
saft or *blart* to a taxi driver
unpacking your bags from his boot.
10 I loved its thick drawl, *g*'s that rang.

Clearing your house, the only thing
I wanted was that box, jemmied open
to let years of lost words spill out –
bibble, fittle, tay, wum,
15 vowels ferrous as nails, consonants

you could lick the coal from.
I wanted to swallow them all: the pits,
railways, factories thunking and clanging
the night shift, the red brick
20 back-to-back you were born in.

I wanted to forge your voice
in my mouth, a blacksmith's furnace;
shout it from the roofs,
send your words, like pigeons,
25 fluttering for home.

This poem is about…

someone from the Black Country – an area in England's West Midlands – who was brought up to hide their regional accent.

How do the first two stanzas present an accent being hidden?

The speaker appears to be addressing a relative. The opening lines establish the extended metaphor of a locked box to convey how the relative hid their accent: 'For years you kept your accent / in a box beneath the bed'. The noun 'box' and the preposition 'beneath' suggest they felt ashamed and didn't want others to know about their background. The box's lock is 'rusted shut', indicating they hid their accent all their life; as rust needs moisture to form, there could be a suggestion that this decision upset them.

Some of the reasons for hiding their accent are depicted in 'hours of **elocution**' and 'teacher's ruler across your legs', showing they were repeatedly taught to speak "correctly" as a child and punished if they made a mistake. Line 4 depicts the teaching of "correct" **vowel sounds** (also known as **received pronunciation**): 'how now brown cow'.

The verb 'escape' in line 6 conveys the relative's negative feelings about their accent through the connotation of keeping it imprisoned. However, this contrasts with the speaker's appreciation – 'I loved its thick drawl' – to indicate how attitudes to accents are changing.

The second stanza features sounds typical of the Black Country accent: 'a **guttural** uh … g's that rang.' The cheerful verb 'rang' reinforces the idea that the speaker approved of their relative's accent. The poem also includes **dialect** words (for daft and cry) in line 8 to suggest regional speech is something unique and interesting that people should be proud of; this is emphasised by including more dialect (for pebble, food, tea and home) in stanza 3.

How do stanzas 3 and 4 present the importance of regional accents?

The third stanza suggests the relative died ('Clearing your house'), having never stopped hiding their accent.

The poet returns to the extended metaphor of the box to explore the speaker's wish to honour the relative by celebrating their background: 'the only thing / I wanted was that box, jemmied open'. The use of 'only' and the forceful verb 'jemmied' suggest the speaker's anger at how the relative was made to feel about their accent. As the extended metaphor continues, there is a tone of both sadness and joy in the speaker's wish to 'let years of lost words spill out' of the box.

The Black Country accent is described in detail, identifying beauty in sounds that some people dislike: the simile 'vowels **ferrous** as nails' presents the accent as strong rather than harsh; the metaphor 'consonants / you could lick the coal from' depicts it as vivid and sensory rather than unpleasant. These images also assert the importance of accent to identity and a sense of place as the Black Country was historically known for its ironworks and coal mining.

This importance is emphasised through the metaphor 'I wanted to swallow them all', displaying an urge to connect with the relative's heritage. A series of landmarks continue the metaphor – 'the pits, / railways, factories … the red brick / back-to-back', with the list building up the assertion that an accent captures where you're from and who you truly are.

How does the final stanza celebrate accent and identity?

The speaker wants to voice the accent that their relative kept hidden – '**forge** your voice / in my mouth'. The blacksmithing metaphors (comparing her mouth to a forge and a furnace) reinforce the link between accent and identity as the smoke from the ironworks was partly how, historically, the Black Country got its name.

The images at the end of the poem link to freedom and release, contrasting with the extended metaphor of the box that was established in the first stanza. The verb phrase 'shout it from the roofs' conveys a desire to celebrate her relative's accent. This is continued in the simile 'send your words, like pigeons, / fluttering for home', which links back to the title and suggests the importance of being connected to your background. There is a sense that the speaker is providing some rest or closure for their dead relative.

How does the poem's form contribute to the way meaning is conveyed?

The stanzas are used to clearly separate the different narrative aspects of the poem.

It is written in free verse and uses a lot of enjambment. This could be to avoid traditional "rules" of poetry, matching the poem's rejection of traditional ideas about how people should speak.

Additional context to consider

Liz Berry was born and raised in the Black Country. Her work often celebrates the area, incorporating its dialect and accent.

The poem appears to be autobiographical; shifting between first and **second person** emphasises the relationship between the speaker and the addressee, even though the latter is now dead.

Accents are sometimes given different statuses. Received Pronunciation is the standard British accent; it is seen by some as the "correct" way to speak and can carry more social prestige.

In the past, the distinctive sounds of the Black Country accent were often perceived in a negative way. Non-standard accents were sometimes seen as a sign of being less educated or of a lower class, leading some people to hide their accents. Until the middle of the 20th century, many schools taught elocution lessons to ensure that pupils spoke "correctly".

While there is still some prejudice today, in the 20th century having a non-standard accent could actually be a barrier to certain careers such as law, finance and the media.

Poetic links

- Connections with places in 'Lines Written in Early Spring', 'England in 1819', 'Shall earth no more inspire thee', 'In a London Drawingroom', 'On an Afternoon Train...', 'pot', 'A Wider View', 'The Jewellery Maker', 'With Birds You're Never Lonely', 'A Portable Paradise' and 'Like an Heiress'.
- Connections between people in 'England in 1819', 'On an Afternoon Train...', 'pot', 'A Wider View', 'A century later', 'With Birds You're Never Lonely' and 'A Portable Paradise'.
- Heritage and identity in 'On an Afternoon Train...', 'Name Journeys', 'pot', 'A Wider View', 'The Jewellery Maker', 'With Birds You're Never Lonely', 'A Portable Paradise', 'Like an Heiress' and 'Thirteen'.
- Personal struggles in 'Shall earth no more inspire thee', 'Name Journeys', 'A Wider View', 'With Birds You're Never Lonely' and 'A Portable Paradise'.

Sample analysis

'Homing' and 'A Portable Paradise' explore how our identities are linked to a sense of place. Berry's poem celebrates the sounds of the Black Country accent through the metaphor 'I wanted to swallow them all: the pits, / railways, factories', conveying how the accent reflects its place of origin. The verb phrase 'swallow them all' suggests a love of the accent and an awareness of its significance in fully understanding one's identity. This is emphasised by the list of local landmarks, building up the suggestion that a person's identity is shaped by where they are from. Similarly, Robinson uses the metaphor 'empty your paradise onto a desk: / your white sands, green hills and fresh fish' to convey how a sense of place helps to secure one's identity and offer support in times of difficulty. The natural images may depict Robinson's Trinidadian heritage; the noun 'paradise' conveys the importance of this to his individual identity which is emphasised by the repetition of 'your'. As with Berry's poem, the list builds up the suggestion that place is an important aspect in the construction of identity.

Questions

QUICK TEST
1. What extended metaphor is important in this poem?
2. What accent does the speaker's relative try to hide?
3. How is this linked to their childhood experiences?
4. How does the speaker feel about their relative's accent?

EXAM PRACTICE
Using one or two of the highlighted quotations to learn, write a paragraph exploring how Berry presents the idea of identity being oppressed.

A century later by Imtiaz Dharker

The school-bell is a call to battle,
every step to class, a step into the firing-line.
Here is the target, fine skin at the temple,
cheek still rounded from being fifteen.

5   Surrendered, surrounded, she
takes the bullet in the head

and walks on. The missile cuts
a pathway in her mind, to an orchard
in full bloom, a field humming under the sun,
10   its lap open and full of poppies.

This girl has won
the right to be ordinary,

wear bangles to a wedding, paint her fingernails,
go to school. Bullet, she says, *you are stupid.*
15   *You have failed.* You cannot kill a book
or the buzzing in it.

A murmur, a swarm. Behind her, one by one,
the schoolgirls are standing up
to take their places on the front line.

This poem is about…

girls' unequal access to education. It was inspired by the experiences of Malala Yousafzai, who was shot by the Taliban at the age of 15 on her way home from school.

How does the first stanza establish the challenges faced by some girls seeking an education?

The schoolgirl can be Malala Yousafzai but can also represent any girl living in a country where women do not have equal access to education.

The opening assertion that 'The school-bell is a call to battle' acknowledges the need to fight for equality and the violent backlash this can bring. The juxtaposition of 'school' and 'battle' is striking because these aspects of life would seem **asynchronous** to people living in a comfortable, equal society. However, Dharker uses alliteration (**bell/battle**) and consonance (bell/battle/school/call) to highlight that, in some countries, these contrasting aspects of life are linked.

The poem has an **ominous** tone and Dharker continues to use seemingly contrasting images to present the dangers that some girls face – 'every step to class, a step into the firing-line'. This time, repetition ('step') is used to emphasise that, for some girls, these different actions are actually linked.

The girl's physical features, 'fine skin … cheek still rounded from being fifteen', emphasise her innocence and vulnerability. This is heightened by referring to her as 'the target'.

How do stanzas 2 and 3 present the attempted murder of the girl?

The girl is described as 'Surrendered', which could suggest she has accepted the danger. Alternatively, it could be interpreted as her being handed over to her attackers, implying a lack of support from the authorities. She is presented as outnumbered ('surrounded'), which adds to the poem's ominous tone. The alliteration and **half-rhyme** link the two words together, emphasising their shared meaning to highlight the girl's vulnerability.

However, an image of bravery is created when she 'takes the bullet in the head' but simply 'walks on'. This metaphor for survival and determination is emphasised by the enjambment across the two stanzas: despite the line break, the sentence continues, just as the girl does.

The metaphor 'The missile cuts / a pathway in her mind' suggests that, instead of killing her, the bullet reveals the need for a better future and makes her more resolute. That future is depicted through natural images, 'an orchard / in full bloom, a field humming under the sun', symbolic of life, unity and happiness. However, the inclusion of 'poppies', a familiar symbol of the commemoration of dead soldiers, suggests that sacrifices will need to be made.

How do the last three stanzas present the determination to win equality of education for girls?

Dharker creates a more triumphant tone when describing how the girl has 'won', in contrast to the 'failed' bullet. This is emphasised by using a list to build up the girl's victories – 'wear bangles to a wedding, paint her fingernails, / go to school'. However, these verb phrases also add to the poem's **pathos** as they seem very commonplace, things that most readers would take for granted.

The girl's confidence and determination is conveyed by her attitude towards the bullet – '*you are stupid. / You have failed.*' Her dismissive tone is emphasised by the short sentences. She also displays a tone of ridicule, '*You cannot kill a book / or the buzzing in it*', presenting knowledge and education as invincible.

Dharker is emphasising the girl's strength and independence by giving her dialogue so her own voice is present in the poem. In contrast, metonymy reduces the girl's oppressors down to a 'stupid' bullet.

The triumphant tone increases by building up images of rebellion. The desire for equal access to education is described as 'A murmur, a swarm', conveying the need for women to speak out and act as a group, with the noun 'swarm' suggesting they can be a strong and dangerous force.

The final image, 'Behind her, one by one, / the schoolgirls are standing up', presents unity and protest. The idea that this is a battle that needs to be fought is emphasised through the return to war imagery: 'take their places on the front line'. However, again, Dharker's words appear to admit that there may be casualties before equality is achieved.

How does the poem's form contribute to the way meaning is conveyed?

The poem does not have a clear stanza structure and is written in free verse. This might be to reflect the poem's themes of freedom and the rebellion against traditional patriarchal structures that oppress women.

> **Additional context to consider**
>
> Dharker was born in Pakistan and brought up in Scotland.
>
> The poem is inspired by Malala Yousafzai who was born in Pakistan and was awarded the Nobel Peace Prize for her education activism. Approximately 50% of the world does not have gender equality in the access to primary education, and this figure rises for secondary education. There are many reasons for this, including oppressive regimes, poverty and gender discrimination within families and schools.
>
> 'A century later' was published in 2014, the centenary of the start of the First World War; it is partly a response to Wilfred Owen's 'Anthem for Doomed Youth' and mirrors the opening of his famous poem: 'What passing-bells for these who die as cattle?'. The association with a war poem reminds the reader of the seriousness of the challenges faced by girls seeking equal access to education.

Poetic links

- Connections between people in 'England in 1819', 'On an Afternoon Train…', 'pot', 'A Wider View', 'Homing', 'With Birds You're Never Lonely' and 'A Portable Paradise'.
- Humankind: conflict, oppression and destruction in 'Lines Written in Early Spring', 'England in 1819', 'In a London Drawingroom', 'Name Journeys', 'pot', 'Homing', 'Like an Heiress' and 'Thirteen'.
- Inequality in 'England in 1819', 'The Jewellery Maker' and 'Thirteen'.
- Hopes and fears in 'A Wider View', 'The Jewellery Maker', 'A Portable Paradise' and 'Thirteen'.

Sample analysis

'A century later' and 'Name Journeys' present conflicts between an individual and society. Inspired by the experience of Malala Yousafzai, Dharker explores a girl's fight for education. When the girl is depicted as 'Surrendered, surrounded, she / takes the bullet in the head / and walks on', it initially creates an ominous tone. She appears alone and outnumbered which makes the violence of the 'bullet in the head' more shocking. However, there is also a sense of victory and determination through the metaphorical use of the verb phrase 'walks on'. This is emphasised by the enjambment, with the lack of pause making her seem resolute and unstoppable. Mundair also makes use of metaphor and violent imagery when conveying her experience of being an immigrant. Her description of being 'chastened / through trial by fire' suggests she felt under attack because of her difference. The verb 'chastened' implies that people belittled or undervalued her and made her feel that she was wrong to try to be part of British society. However, like in Dharker's poem, there is a suggestion of determination through the image of a 'trial by fire', indicating that she was treated harshly but ultimately proved herself.

Questions

QUICK TEST
1. What is the girl in the poem seeking?
2. What is the tone of the opening stanzas?
3. How does the tone change in the second half of the poem?
4. What similar imagery is used in the first and last stanzas?

EXAM PRACTICE
Using one or two of the highlighted quotations to learn, write a paragraph exploring how Dharker presents oppression.

The Jewellery Maker
by Louisa Adjoa Parker

Each day after sunrise he walks to the workshop
– like his father before him, and his father too –
the slap of sandalled feet on heat-baked stone,
the smell of blossom, a plate-blue sky. He greets
5 his neighbours with a smile. In the distance
a wild dog barks.

He sits straight-backed, lays out pointed tools
the way a surgeon might – neat as soldiers.
He likes hot metal, the smell, the way it yields
10 to his touch. Under deft fingers gold butterflies dance;
flowers bloom; silvery moons wax and wane,
then wax again; bright dragonflies flap two pairs of wings.

He likes the tiny loops and curls – he'd decorate
his house in this, drape his wife in fine-spun gold;
15 her skin wrinkled by sun, in simple cotton dress,
her only jewellery a plain gold band, worn thin.
He imagines the women who will wear
what he has made, clear-eyed, bird-boned, unlined skin
warming the metal his hands caress.

This poem is about…

a man who has followed in his family's footsteps to work as a jeweller; he enjoys his work but doesn't make much money.

How does the first stanza present identity and place?

Jewellery making is presented as part of the character's heritage – 'like his father before him, and his father too', with the repetition suggesting the idea of family lineage. This could also link to the economic necessity of learning a skill from his father.

The description of his mornings, 'Each day after sunrise he walks to the workshop', includes references to time and routine to indicate his commitment to his work; the suggestion that this regular early start might also be tiring is increased by the verb 'walks'. He is going to 'the' workshop, not 'his' workshop, implying that he works for others and therefore does not necessarily receive the full value of his labours.

The poem's setting is unspecified but it is described through different senses. The references to sight ('a plate-blue sky'), smell ('blossom') and touch ('heat-baked stone') evoke a hot, beautiful region, while the sounds ('the slap of sandalled feet … a wild dog barks') might imply a lack of wealth. Alliteration (s and b) helps to link these images to build up a vivid impression of the man's life.

The use of the senses also suggests how much he feels connected to this place which is reinforced by the simple description of his happiness: 'He greets / his neighbours with a smile.'

How does stanza 2 present the man's approach to his work?

The man's professionalism is indicated through physical descriptions of him. He 'sits straight-backed', indicating seriousness, while the description of his '**deft** fingers' suggests he works skilfully and neatly.

This is developed through the description of his approach to his work. When he 'lays out pointed tools / the way a surgeon might', the comparison to a 'surgeon' indicates his expertise and precision while the verb 'lays' suggests time and care. This is reinforced by the simile about his tools, 'neat as soldiers', suggesting an exact and methodical approach to his work.

His talent is conveyed through metaphor in lines 10–12: 'gold butterflies dance; / flowers bloom; silvery moons wax and wane, / then wax again; bright dragonflies flap'. The different verbs make his jewellery seem alive, indicating the detail and accuracy of his work. The descriptions are built up by the list to emphasise his abilities. Additionally, the use of natural imagery could suggest that jewellery making is part of the man's nature, relating to how the opening lines linked it to his heritage.

His enjoyment of his work is conveyed through different senses: 'He likes hot metal, the smell, the way it yields / to his touch.' The verb 'yields' shows how he has mastery over his jewellery work while the tricolon builds up his satisfaction.

How does the final stanza develop the reader's impression of the jewellery maker's life?

Stanza 3 suggests the jewellery maker struggles financially, adding a tone of disappointment to the poem.

His wife is depicted as wearing 'simple' clothes. She also has 'only' one piece of jewellery which is a 'plain gold band, worn thin', the two adjectives contrasting with the vivid metaphors about his jewellery making in the previous stanza. Additionally, she is 'wrinkled by sun', implying she works outdoors, presumably for low pay.

These images of a simple life contrast with the description of the 'loops and curls' with which he would like to 'decorate / his house', indicating his wish to make their life better. Similarly, he would like to 'drape his wife in fine-spun gold' compared to the 'simple cotton' she is used to.

Comparisons are created between his wife and the women who will wear his jewellery (presumably the wives of wealthier men). The description of them as 'clear-eyed, bird-boned, unlined skin' conveys freshness, fragility and calm. The tricolon builds these images up to suggest they have an easier life than his own wife, perhaps implying he feels guilty at not being able to provide better for his family.

The final line – 'warming the metal his hands caress' – juxtaposes verbs with different connotations. While 'warming' suggests the heat of the wearer's body passing into the jewellery, 'caress' is much more active, loving and intimate. This implies that his work will never mean as much to the wearer as it means to him (perhaps because of their wealth and amount of jewellery).

How does the poem's form contribute to the way meaning is conveyed?

The three stanzas separate different aspects of the man's life.

The poem is written in free verse with some enjambment, perhaps to mirror the creative art of the jewellery maker.

However, it also contains a lot of **caesura**, interrupting the sense of rhythm in the lines; this might relate to how his life isn't as happy and free as it at first seems (perhaps due to the financial struggles that are implied).

Additional context to consider

Parker is a writer of English and Ghanaian heritage who is interested in telling the stories of **marginalised** voices. This may be why the jewellery maker and his location remain unnamed: people often don't think about who makes their jewellery and, additionally, the man could be representing lots of similar workers.

Throughout the poem, the writer focuses on small details. This style of writing matches the man's occupation and can also be used to humanise "unknown" figures or make them seem more "real".

Poetic links

- Connections with places in 'Lines Written in Early Spring', 'England in 1819', 'Shall earth no more inspire thee', 'In a London Drawingroom', 'On an Afternoon Train…', 'pot', 'A Wider View', 'Homing', 'With Birds You're Never Lonely', 'A Portable Paradise' and 'Like an Heiress'.
- Heritage and identity in 'On an Afternoon Train…', 'Name Journeys', 'pot', 'A Wider View', 'Homing', 'With Birds You're Never Lonely', 'A Portable Paradise', 'Like an Heiress' and 'Thirteen'.
- Inequality in 'England in 1819', 'A century later' and 'Thirteen'.
- Hopes and fears in 'A Wider View', 'A century later', 'A Portable Paradise' and 'Thirteen'.

Sample analysis

'The Jewellery Maker' and 'Lines Written in Early Spring' use a range of senses to present how a place can bring happiness. Parker describes the man's experience of walking to work as being almost idyllic: 'feet on heat-baked stone, / the smell of blossom, a plate-blue sky. He greets / his neighbours with a smile.' Through touch, smell and sight, Parker evokes the warmth and beauty of the man's surroundings. His resultant happiness is conveyed through the verb 'greets' and the noun 'smile'. Wordsworth makes similar use of senses when describing a wood in springtime: 'I heard a thousand blended notes … Through primrose tufts, in that green **bower**'. The Romantic poets often found inspiration in nature and his depiction of birdsong suggests personal joy in how harmonious everything seems. Additionally, the adjective 'green' conveys how wonderfully alive and natural the wood is, perhaps contrasting with – and providing a relief from – the increased industrialisation and urbanisation that concerned Wordsworth at the time.

Questions

QUICK TEST
1. How is simile used to show the care the jewellery maker takes at work?
2. What technique is used to show his creative talents as a jeweller?
3. What would the jewellery maker like to be able to do?
4. How is his wife compared to the women who will wear the jewellery that he makes?

EXAM PRACTICE
Using one or two of the highlighted quotations to learn, write a paragraph exploring how Parker presents a contrast between the rich and the poor.

With Birds You're Never Lonely
by Raymond Antrobus

I can't hear the barista
over the coffee machine.

Spoons slam, steam rises.
I catch the eye of a man

5   sitting in the corner
of the cafe reading alone

about trees which is, incidentally,
all I can think about

since returning.
10 Last week I sat alone

on a stump, deep in Zelandia forest
with sun-syrupped Kauri trees

and brazen Tui birds with white tufts
and yellow and black beaks.

15 They landed by my feet, blaring so loudly
I had to turn off my hearing aids.

When all sound disappeared, I was tuned
into a silence that was not an absence.

As I switched sound on again,
20 silence collapsed.

The forest spat all the birds back,
and I was jealous—

the earthy Kauri trees, their endless
brown and green trunks of sturdiness.

25 I wondered what the trees
would say about us?

What books would they write
if they had to cut us down?

Later, stumbling from the forest I listened
30 to a young Maori woman.

She could tell which bird chirped,
a skill she learned from her grandfather

who said *with birds you're never lonely*.
In that moment I felt sorry

35 for any grey tree in London,
for the family they don't have,

the Gods they can't hold.

This poem is about...

the ways in which we interact and connect with others and our environments, explored through a deaf person's experience of the urban and natural worlds.

How do lines 1–10 present interactions within the urban world?

The poem begins with a deaf person's experience of a coffee shop, describing how secondary noise makes it difficult for him to communicate: 'I can't hear the **barista** / over the coffee machine'. The simple language reflects how he faces obstacles even in basic situations like ordering a coffee. The verb phrases 'Spoons slam, steam rises' highlight the intrusive sounds; the sibilance links the words together, conveying how these noises build up into something that is, **aurally**, overwhelming.

Communication is also presented as being non-verbal, perhaps because this is less of an obstacle for the deaf person – 'I catch the eye of a man'. The other customer appears to have a similar wish for quiet to the speaker because he is 'sitting in the corner ... alone'; this unspoken connection might also imply that the speaker sometimes feels excluded from society due to his deafness. They also have a shared but unspoken interest as the other customer is reading a book 'about trees which is, incidentally, / all I can think about'. The adverb 'incidentally' is perhaps suggesting that our connections with others can sometimes be completely random.

The first half of the fifth couplet is set in the coffeehouse while the second half, as if prompted by the man's book about trees, begins the speaker's recollection of his time in a Zelandia forest. The poet is using structure to emphasise unspoken connections between people. This is highlighted by the repetition of the adjective 'alone' from line 6, suggesting these two strangers have been in similar (yet geographically very different) situations.

How do lines 11–18 present interactions with the natural world?

The forest is initially presented as beautiful through the use of the metaphor 'sun-syrupped Kauri trees', making everything sound golden and full of light.

Colour is also used to present the wildlife as captivating – 'Tui birds with white tufts / and yellow and black beaks'. However, the birds are also noisy – 'blaring so loudly' – which relates back to his experience in the coffeeshop. The verb 'blaring' suggests an unnecessarily harsh sound and this is emphasised by the intensifier and adverb, making it seem overwhelming.

The way the birds are described – 'brazen ... They landed by my feet' – could increase the impression that he feels almost attacked by the sound. This is reinforced by the modal verb in the next line, 'I had to turn off my hearing aids', indicating that he had no choice.

However, as in the coffeeshop, he experiences another unexpected connection: 'I was tuned / into a silence that was not an absence.' This time, he discovers a link with nature which is presented as a powerful presence (rather than an 'absence'). The verb phrase 'tuned / into' suggests the speaker comes into harmony with nature and feels peaceful.

How do lines 19–28 explore connections with the natural world?

The speaker uses a metaphor to convey how the return of sound causes discomfort, 'silence collapsed', which again links to his experience in the coffee shop. This is emphasised through personification, 'The forest spat all the birds back', suggesting that he feels assaulted and overwhelmed by sound.

The speaker admits that he felt 'jealous' and found a connection with the unhearing trees of the forest. He describes them as 'earthy Kauri trees, their endless / brown and green trunks of sturdiness', indicating that he is impressed by their size and strength. The adjectives 'earthy' and 'brown and green' might also suggest that he envies their sense of place and how they fit into, or even dominate, the forest.

He then reflects philosophically on humankind's relationship with nature, wondering what the trees 'would say about us'. The inclusion of the pronoun 'us' adds another connection, in terms of the speaker's place in humanity. He considers how we destroy nature and whether nature would do the same – 'What books would they write / if they had to cut us down?'. These ideas are perhaps presented through rhetorical questions because the answers are unknowable.

How do lines 29–37 continue to explore interactions and connections?

The speaker's experience appears to have left him disturbed as he describes himself 'stumbling from the forest', as if trying to escape. Additionally, the verb 'stumbling' could refer to communication and how he struggles to convey what he thought and felt in the forest.

He describes meeting a 'young Maori woman'. The importance of sound in communication is reiterated by the fact that he 'listened' to her. He is impressed by her ability to distinguish between the sounds of each communicating bird, 'She could tell which bird chirped', in contrast to how he has found himself overwhelmed by sounds.

This 'skill' is part of her heritage, 'learned from her grandfather'. The idea of passing down experience is emphasised by her repeating her grandfather's words, 'with birds you're never lonely'. There is perhaps some pathos here as, due to the speaker's hearing problems, he did not have this comforting experience with the birds.

The grandfather's words create another connection, this time to the trees in London. He feels 'sorry' for the trees which are described as 'grey' and without 'family', perhaps relating the lack of birds to increased urbanisation or pollution. Alternatively, after feeling excluded and attacked by the sound of the birds, he could be comparing himself to the unhappy London trees.

The final line, 'the Gods they can't hold', may suggest that humankind doesn't respect nature enough: we see ourselves as the gods rather than seeing wonder in the world around us. Again, alternatively, he could be comparing himself to the empty, soundless trees and reflecting on the challenges of being a deaf person in a world that worships sound.

How does the poem's form contribute to the way meaning is conveyed?

The use of couplets highlights the poem's repeated motif of things connecting.

Contrasting with the fixed arrangement of couplets, the poem is written in free verse. This could reflect the differences within which the poet is finding connections. Alternatively, the free verse could link to how he depicts the world around him, due to his issues with sound, as seeming slightly uncontrolled or chaotic.

The poet uses a lot of enjambment in the poem, emphasising connections by not separating them with punctuation. By building up descriptions of sound without pauses or separation, the enjambment could also reflect how the speaker finds noises overwhelming.

Additional context to consider

Raymond Antrobus was diagnosed as deaf at age six. He has English and Jamaican heritage, and often explores themes of communication, connection and cultural inheritance.

Deaf charities often cite how little our predominantly hearing society understands the experiences of those with hearing issues (some people are born deaf, while others develop hearing issues later in life), including their unequal access to services and education.

The poem is written in the first person and is autobiographical with an **anecdotal** style, creating greater intimacy with the reader. This is important as the poem is partly about understanding the deaf experience. The combination of past and present tense links to the poem's exploration of how events and experiences in our lives are connected.

Poetic links

- The natural world in 'Lines Written in Early Spring', 'Shall earth no more inspire thee', 'A Portable Paradise' and 'Like an Heiress'.
- Connections with places in 'Lines Written in Early Spring', 'England in 1819', 'Shall earth no more inspire thee', 'In a London Drawingroom', 'On an Afternoon Train...', 'pot', 'A Wider View', 'Homing', 'The Jewellery Maker', 'A Portable Paradise' and 'Like an Heiress'.
- Connections between people in 'England in 1819', 'On an Afternoon Train...', 'pot', 'A Wider View', 'Homing', 'A century later' and 'A Portable Paradise'.
- Heritage and identity in 'On an Afternoon Train...', 'Name Journeys', 'pot', 'A Wider View', 'Homing', 'The Jewellery Maker', 'A Portable Paradise', 'Like an Heiress' and 'Thirteen'.
- Personal struggles in 'Shall earth no more inspire thee', 'Name Journeys', 'A Wider View', 'Homing' and 'A Portable Paradise'.

Sample analysis

'With Birds You're Never Lonely' and 'Shall earth no more inspire thee' present different responses to the natural world. Antrobus describes the birds in the Zelandia forest as 'blaring so loudly / I had to turn off my hearing aids', giving the impression that he feels under attack. The verb 'blaring' makes the sound of the birds seem unnecessarily harsh and this is emphasised by the intensifier and adverb. As a deaf person, sound is amplified by his hearing aids so heightened noises are overwhelming. The modal verb 'had' relates to this by depicting how he feels forced to respond. In contrast, Brontë's poem presents a much more comforting view of nature. The lines 'I know my mountain breezes / Enchant and soothe thee still' suggest that nature heals rather than attacks. Like Antrobus's poem, this is conveyed through verbs: 'soothe' suggests calmness while 'enchant' implies something magically distracting. The overall impression of nature as comforting is emphasised by Brontë using the form of a dramatic monologue, from the point of view of nature, so it appears to be directly reassuring the reader.

Questions

QUICK TEST
1. What does the speaker find difficult in the coffee shop?
2. What does the other coffee shop customer make him think about?
3. What does he have to do in the forest because of the birds?
4. What does he feel about the trees in the forest?

EXAM PRACTICE
Using one or two of the highlighted quotations to learn, write a paragraph exploring how Antrobus presents personal struggles.

A Portable Paradise
by Roger Robinson

And if I speak of Paradise,
then I'm speaking of my grandmother
who told me to carry it always
on my person, concealed, so
5 no one else would know but me.
That way they can't steal it, she'd say.
And if life puts you under pressure,
trace its ridges in your pocket,
smell its piney scent on your handkerchief,
10 hum its anthem under your breath.
And if your stresses are sustained and daily,
get yourself to an empty room – be it hotel,
hostel or hovel – find a lamp
and empty your paradise onto a desk:
15 your white sands, green hills and fresh fish.
Shine the lamp on it like the fresh hope
of morning, and keep staring at it till you sleep.

This poem is about…

how strong connections to one's heritage, through memories of places and people, can be comforting during times of stress or unhappiness.

How does the poem establish an extended metaphor?

The extended metaphor of a 'portable paradise' is used throughout the poem to represent something that brings comfort. In the first two lines, the speaker links 'Paradise' to his grandmother, suggesting his source of comfort is an **abstract** idea that connects him to places and people. This is reinforced in line 15 when his personal paradise is described as 'white sands, green hills and fresh fish'. The poem appears autobiographical so these images suggest his specific paradise is his Trinidadian heritage and the memory of his childhood there.

How do lines 3–6 present the importance of a 'portable paradise'?

His grandmother's advice that he should 'carry it always / on my person' uses the adverb 'always' to show its importance to his life. The noun phrase 'my person' also implies that being in touch with his heritage is a significant part of his sense of identity and wellbeing.

This importance is reinforced by the idea that it should be kept 'concealed, so … they can't steal it'. The adjective 'concealed' and the verb 'steal' indicate something personally precious or of great value. The links to identity are emphasised through the wish that 'no one else would know but me', creating a sense of intimacy and privacy.

However, this could also imply that he feels the need to hide his identity from other people for fear it will not be respected. This perhaps links to how societies sometimes encourage cultural **assimilation** rather than celebrating people's different heritages.

How do lines 7–15 present the benefits of a 'portable paradise'?

From line 7 onwards, the poet starts to use the second person, 'you', and many imperatives. This could be the speaker recalling his grandmother's words or he could be directly addressing the reader, to encourage us to form our own 'portable paradise'. The passing on of wisdom is significant to the poem's themes as it is another way in which heritage is shaped.

The poem acknowledges how 'life puts you under pressure'. The personification of daily life makes it seem more stressful as it depicts a physical entity that can weigh us down. This is emphasised by referring to how 'stresses are sustained and daily', using the two adjectives to indicate a constant pressure. The poet could be describing general stresses or, relating to his own background, the challenges and obstacles of being Black British.

By using a list of nouns with decreasing status, 'hotel, / hostel or **hovel**', the poet could be linking stress to financial difficulties or acknowledging that anyone can struggle in life, regardless of their wealth or social status.

Lines 8–10 use the extended metaphor to depict the soothing of problems, 'trace its ridges in your pocket, / smell its piney scent on your handkerchief, / hum its anthem under your breath', incorporating touch, smell and sound to convey a more evocative, sensory connection with one's heritage. The use of senses implies that such an awareness can be invigorating. All the verbs (trace, smell, hum) are gentle, reinforcing the idea of comfort, while the noun 'anthem' might also be significant as it suggests pride and togetherness. The tricolon builds up these images to convey how small, beautiful things can have a powerful, overall impact on life.

A Portable Paradise

Lines 13–15 continue to use the extended metaphor to present a way to cope with life's problems: 'find a lamp / and empty your paradise onto a desk'. The image of the lamp is used to suggest immersing oneself in one's heritage. The natural images of 'your white sands, green hills and fresh fish' suggest calm and comfort while the possessive pronoun 'your' creates a sense of proud ownership and of feeling whole.

How does the end of the poem present the importance of identity?

The need to explore, understand and feel proud of one's heritage is conveyed in the final imperatives, 'Shine the lamp on it ... keep staring at it'. The verbs 'shine' and 'staring' suggest how important this connection is to our identities. The simile 'like the fresh hope / of morning' suggests such a connection to one's heritage can be a source of inner-strength and **optimism**. Similarly, the final reference to 'sleep' implies it can bring inner peace and calm.

How does the poem's form contribute to the way meaning is conveyed?

The poem is written to resemble a conversation, particularly through the use of the second person ('you'). Additionally, by starting with a **conjunction** ('And'), the first line seems to begin mid-sentence; this technique is repeated in lines 7 and 11. Written in free verse, the rhythms of the lines also seem closer to natural speech than formal poetry.

Additional context to consider

Roger Robinson's parents were from Trinidad. He was born in London but the family returned home after his birth. He grew up in Trinidad and returned to England when he was nineteen, initially living with his grandmother. The poem appears to be autobiographical and is partly written in the first person, alluding to the challenges he faced in England and how he was helped by the advice of his grandmother.

Most of the poem is the grandmother's voice (to emphasise the significance of her advice) and uses the second person to address Robinson. This creates a sense of intimacy and allows her message to be aimed at the reader, acknowledging that everyone has individual problems that can be helped by feeling more secure in their own identity.

Poetic links

- The natural world in 'Lines Written in Early Spring', 'Shall earth no more inspire thee', 'With Birds You're Never Lonely' and 'Like an Heiress'.
- Connections with places in 'Lines Written in Early Spring', 'England in 1819', 'Shall earth no more inspire thee', 'In a London Drawingroom', 'On an Afternoon Train...', 'pot', 'A Wider View', 'Homing', 'The Jewellery Maker', 'With Birds You're Never Lonely' and 'Like an Heiress'.

- Connections between people in 'England in 1819', 'On an Afternoon Train...', 'pot', 'A Wider View', 'Homing', 'A century later' and 'With Birds You're Never Lonely'.
- Heritage and identity in 'On an Afternoon Train...', 'Name Journeys', 'pot', 'A Wider View', 'Homing', 'The Jewellery Maker', 'With Birds You're Never Lonely', 'Like an Heiress' and 'Thirteen'.
- Immigration in 'Name Journeys' and 'A Wider View'.
- Personal struggles in 'Shall earth no more inspire thee', 'Name Journeys', 'A Wider View', 'Homing' and 'With Birds You're Never Lonely'.
- Hopes and fears in 'A Wider View', 'A century later', 'The Jewellery Maker' and 'Thirteen'.

Sample analysis

'A Portable Paradise' and 'In a London Drawingroom' present life as oppressive. Perhaps drawing on his experience of coming to England as a nineteen-year-old, Robinson describes how 'life puts you under pressure ... your stresses are sustained and daily', using the nouns 'pressure' and 'stresses' to convey difficulties. This is emphasised by personifying life, making it seem like a physical entity that deliberately weighs people down, and using the adjectives 'sustained' and 'daily' to suggest that such problems are relentless. In comparison, Eliot presents the pressures of life through hyperbole. Comparing society to 'one huge prison-house & court', she creates a similar sense of relentlessness, implying that everyone is trapped in their daily routines. The reference to a 'court' suggests this is worsened by people feeling constantly judged, whether legally or socially.

Questions

QUICK TEST
1. Who taught the speaker about having a 'portable paradise'?
2. How is it meant to help the speaker?
3. What technique is the poet using with the idea of a 'portable paradise'?
4. What does the speaker's personal 'paradise' appear to be?

EXAM PRACTICE
Using one or two of the highlighted quotations to learn, write a paragraph exploring how Robinson presents connections with places as being comforting.

Like an Heiress by Grace Nichols

Like an heiress, drawn to the light of her
eye-catching jewels, Atlantic draws me
to the mirror of my oceanic small-days.
But the beach is deserted except for a lone
5 wave of rubbish against the old seawall –
used car tyres, plastic bottles, styrofoam cups –
rightly tossed back by an ocean's moodswings.
Undisturbed, not even by a seabird,
I stand under the sun's burning treasury
10 gazing out at the far-out gleam of Atlantic,
before heading back like a tourist
to the sanctuary of my hotel room
to dwell in the air-conditioned coolness
on the quickening years and fate of our planet.

This poem is about…
the speaker returning to their homeland to find it ruined by pollution.

How do the first three lines present the idea of returning home?

The poet is from Guyana and originally lived in a small coastal village; she moved to Britain as an adult. The opening simile, 'Like an heiress', summarises her appreciation of her Guyanese heritage. The comparison to an **'heiress'** suggests she feels she has inherited something valuable; this richness is meant in terms of its impact on her identity rather than monetary worth.

This is emphasised by the metaphor comparing Guyana to 'eye-catching jewels', again suggesting beauty and worth. When she describes being 'drawn to the light' of Guyana, 'light' symbolises ideas of hope and happiness (and is possibly a joke about contrastingly bad British weather). The verb 'drawn' implies she feels connected to her homeland and that there is a natural instinct to return.

Another metaphor, 'the mirror of my oceanic small-days', suggests a wish to revisit her childhood when she lived by the ocean. The noun phrase 'small-days' refers to being a child, conveying innocence and simplicity before the responsibilities of adulthood; alternatively, it could suggest life in Guyana is calmer than in Britain. Her use of the noun 'mirror' implies she expected everything to look the same as when she was a child.

How do lines 4–7 present the reality of returning home?

Starting the sentence with the conjunction 'But' indicates a problem and these lines develop a tone of disappointment or disillusionment. The reference to the beach being 'deserted' indicates it is no longer a happy, pleasant place where people want to be.

Humankind's destructive impact on the natural world is presented in the image of 'a lone / wave of rubbish', using metaphor to replace nature with waste. This is the only thing she sees, conveyed through the adjective 'lone', implying the rubbish has driven everyone away. Noun phrases illustrate the different kinds of rubbish, 'car tyres, plastic bottles, styrofoam cups', with the tricolon building up the scale of the pollution.

Poets often use personification to indicate the importance of something or its equality with humankind. The ocean is given 'moodswings' to describe the ebb and flow of the tide, indicating that nature is unhappy with the pollution. This is emphasised by the ocean having 'rightly tossed back' the rubbish; the adverb asserts that we shouldn't be polluting nature while the verb phrase 'tossed back' suggests such waste has no place in the waters.

How does the second half of the poem explore the speaker's feelings?

Line 8 creates a sense of absence, adding to the tone of disappointment. The speaker is 'Undisturbed, not even by a seabird', linking to line 4's adjective 'deserted'. The lack of birds suggests the wider effects of pollution.

This may also be implied by the metaphor 'the sun's burning treasury'. While it could describe the beautiful weather, it can also be an allusion to rising global temperatures. Similarly, the image of her 'gazing out at the far-out gleam of Atlantic' could suggest tranquillity through the relaxed verb 'gazing' and the brightness of the noun 'gleam'. However, this depiction of her staring at the horizon might represent her helplessly considering the planet's future.

Whereas she compared herself to an 'heiress' in line 1, the poet uses the much less contented simile 'like a tourist' in line 11. This implies Guyana is no longer how she remembered it; she does not feel a strong connection to it anymore. The description of returning to her hotel emphasises the idea of feeling like an outsider: the verb phrase 'heading back' suggests a wish to escape and the noun 'sanctuary' reinforces this, implying she now feels more of a connection with the hotel than she does with Guyana.

The poem ends on a **pessimistic** tone. The speaker considers 'the quickening years and fate of our planet', using the noun 'fate' to acknowledge that climate change cannot be reversed while the adjective 'quickening' suggests environmental destruction is getting ever closer.

Concern for the environment is juxtaposed with the speaker contributing to global warming. The reference to 'air-conditioned coolness' acknowledges her own complicity in the problem, opting for personal comfort over reducing climate change. The safe, comfortable hotel room may be a metaphor for how humankind is ignoring or accepting the planet's problems rather than trying to solve them.

How does the poem's form contribute to the way meaning is conveyed?

The poem is written as a sonnet, a familiar form of love poetry, which matches her feelings about Guyana and the natural world. This also increases the surprise for the reader when the positive tone changes after line 3.

In a sonnet, the **volta** (or turn of thought) comes towards the end; Nichols does not follow this tradition, just as her sonnet is written in free verse rather than iambic pentameter with structured rhyme. This could be seen as an expression of her Guyanese heritage (rebelling against traditional poetic structures in the same way the country rebelled against colonial structures).

> ### Additional context to consider
>
> Grace Nichols was born in British Guiana in 1950. Guyana regained its independence in 1966 and Nichols moved to Britain in 1977.
>
> The poem is autobiographical, forming part of a sonnet cycle that was inspired by a return visit to Guyana.
>
> The destruction of the environment is a universal problem. Although writing in the first person, the poet maintains a shared interest by using familiar images of types and causes of pollution.

Poetic links

- The natural world in 'Lines Written in Early Spring', 'Shall earth no more inspire thee', 'With Birds You're Never Lonely' and 'A Portable Paradise'.
- The urban world and pollution in 'In a London Drawingroom' and 'A Wider View'.
- Connections with places in 'Lines Written in Early Spring', 'England in 1819', 'Shall earth no more inspire thee', 'In a London Drawingroom', 'On an Afternoon Train…', 'pot', 'A Wider View', 'Homing', 'The Jewellery Maker', 'With Birds You're Never Lonely' and 'A Portable Paradise'.
- Heritage and identity in 'On an Afternoon Train…', 'Name Journeys', 'pot', 'A Wider View', 'Homing', 'The Jewellery Maker', 'With Birds You're Never Lonely', 'A Portable Paradise' and 'Thirteen'.
- Humankind: conflict, oppression and destruction in 'Lines Written in Early Spring', 'England in 1819', 'In a London Drawingroom', 'Name Journeys', 'pot', 'Homing', 'A century later' and 'Thirteen'.

Sample analysis

'Like an Heiress' and 'Homing' present the speakers' appreciation of their heritage. Nichols's metaphor 'drawn to the light of her / eye-catching jewels' conveys a positive connection to her homeland of Guyana. The jewellery image suggests she values her heritage and is proud to show it off. The 'light' symbolises how her heritage brings her happiness and perhaps a stronger understanding of her identity, while the verb 'drawn' conveys how returning to her birthplace feels instinctual. Berry's poem is similarly autobiographical and focuses on how she values her Black Country heritage. Like Nichols, she uses a metaphor to convey her pride – 'I wanted to forge your voice / in my mouth, a blacksmith's furnace; / shout it from the roofs' – and this is particularly evident in the second verb phrase. The images of blacksmithing link to the region's history, suggesting a similar wish to connect with the past. However, these lines have more pathos as she is also reflecting on a relative who felt ashamed of their heritage.

Questions

QUICK TEST
1. What form of poetry has been used for 'Like an Heiress'?
2. What is the setting of the poem?
3. How is the setting different from what the poet expected?
4. How does the tone of the poem change?

EXAM PRACTICE
Using one or two of the highlighted quotations to learn, write a paragraph exploring how Nichols presents the pollution of the natural world.

Like an Heiress

Thirteen by Caleb Femi

You will be four minutes from home
when you are cornered by an officer
who will tell you of a robbery, forty
minutes ago in the area. *You fit*
5 *the description of a man?* – You'll laugh.
Thirteen, you'll tell him: you're thirteen.

You'll be patted on the shoulder, then, by another fed
whose face takes you back to Gloucester Primary School,
a Wednesday assembly about *being little stars*.
10 This same officer had an horizon in the east
of his smile when he told your class that
you were all *supernovas*,
the *biggest* and *brightest stars*.

You will show the warmth of your teeth
15 praying he remembers the heat of your supernova;
he will see you powerless – plump.
You will watch the two men cast lots for your organs.

Don't you remember me? you will ask.
You gave a talk at my primary school.
20 While fear condenses on your lips,
you will remember that Wednesday, after the assembly,
your teacher speaking more about supernovas:
how they are, in fact, dying stars
on the verge of becoming black holes.

This poem is about…
a young person's experience of systemic racism.

How does the first stanza establish the situation?
The poem makes immediate use of the second person, 'You', suggesting that systemic racism is a shared experience for Black people. This is reinforced by the repetition of the modal verb 'will', indicating something definite.

Shifts in tone are used to present the boy being victimised by the police. The initial image of safety, 'You will be four minutes from home', is followed by an image of threat, 'when you are cornered by an officer'. The verb 'cornered' makes the boy seem vulnerable, suggesting no escape; the use of the noun 'officer' adds a disturbing tone as the police are meant to protect. The repetition of the boy's age in line 6 indicates his desperation to be believed.

In lines 4–5, the idea of the boy being 'thirteen' yet mistaken for 'a man' seems ridiculous and this is emphasised by the rhetorical question and the subsequent phrase, 'You'll laugh.' However, the verb phrase 'fit / the description' displays systemic racism because all the police officer sees is the colour of the boy's skin.

How does the second stanza present hypocrisy?
The poet juxtaposes the present-day situation with a seemingly more positive experience from the past to convey the **hypocrisy** of the police service.

Although the verb 'patted' could sound gentle, the differences in age and authority create a suggestion of physical intimidation; this is emphasised by the adjective 'another' because the boy is outnumbered. "Pat" can also mean to check for concealed items, linking to how they suspect the boy is a criminal.

The boy recognises the officer from a primary school assembly. The officer's positive language about the children – '*little stars*', '*supernovas*', the '*biggest* and *brightest stars*' – creates a tone of irony. Despite the repeated symbolism of light suggesting hope and happiness, and the superlatives indicating respect and success, the boy has now been suspected of a crime based on his racial appearance. The officer's past words seem like **insincere** hyperbole, suggesting the police service only pretends to care about and believe in young people.

Similarly, the metaphor about the officer ('had an horizon in the east / of his smile') implies optimism and friendliness by comparing his smile to a sunrise. However, this seems ironic when the two scenes are juxtaposed, reinforcing the hypocrisy by suggesting that his positive attitude was not genuine.

By replacing the formal noun 'officer' with the slang term 'fed', the poet could be indicating that this experience causes the boy to lose respect for the police.

How does the third stanza present an imbalance of power?

The boy's nervousness is conveyed in 'praying he remembers the heat of your supernova'. The verb 'praying' shows his desperation to be believed and considered innocent. However, these hopes are made to seem **futile** by using the 'supernova' metaphor, referring back to the previous stanza and the police officer's lack of genuine belief in young people.

The boy tries to appear friendly by smiling, 'the warmth of your teeth', and wants to show that he is harmless, 'powerless – plump'. The second image builds up the poem's disturbing tone as it can also be interpreted as the officers enjoying the boy's vulnerability; the adjective 'plump' often describes meat and fruit that looks tasty, implying the police officers see the boy as their prey. This is developed by the metaphor 'the two men cast lots for your organs', suggesting police brutality and conveying the speaker's dread.

How does the final stanza present fear?

The boy's terror is conveyed through the metaphor 'fear condenses on your lips'. By comparing his fear to sweat, it suggests the emotion is so strong that it is coming out of his pores. This is emphasised by the desperate tone of his speech, *'Don't you remember me?'*.

The final lines of the poem add further irony to the police officer's words in assembly by reminding the reader that supernovas are 'dying stars' that will become 'black holes'. These images act as a metaphor for the boy's fear about what the police officers might do to him. They might also imply how the experience changes his outlook on life: he loses positivity, perhaps seeing himself as worthless or now hating the establishment.

Using astronomical imagery and the noun 'verge' (the final point before something happens) might also link to the concept of fate, relating to the theme of systemic racism by suggesting this was always going to happen to the boy at some point due to the colour of his skin.

How does the poem's form contribute to the way meaning is conveyed?

The poem is written in free verse and features enjambment, increasing its resemblance to natural, everyday speech. This could be to highlight the situation's realism and regularity.

Enjambment creates fewer pauses in a poem because the lines "run-on" rather than being end-stopped. The poet could be doing this to reflect the idea that Black people can't avoid systemic racism or how it seems unstoppable.

Additional context to consider

Caleb Femi was born in Nigeria but moved to Britain when he was seven. He grew up on London's North Peckham Estate which gained notoriety after the murder of Damilola Taylor, a ten-year-old Nigerian boy.

This is an autobiographical poem, detailing a personal experience. The second person and future tense present systemic racism as a typical situation for Black people as well as encouraging White readers to empathise with the experience of discrimination.

Poetic links

- Heritage and identity in 'On an Afternoon Train…', 'Name Journeys', 'pot', 'A Wider View', 'Homing', 'The Jewellery Maker', 'With Birds You're Never Lonely', 'A Portable Paradise' and 'Like an Heiress'.
- Humankind: conflict, oppression and destruction in 'Lines Written in Early Spring', 'England in 1819', 'In a London Drawingroom', 'Name Journeys', 'pot', 'Homing', 'A century later' and 'Like an Heiress'.
- Inequality in 'England in 1819', 'A century later' and 'The Jewellery Maker'.
- Hopes and fears in 'A Wider View', 'A century later', 'The Jewellery Maker' and 'A Portable Paradise'.

Sample analysis

'Thirteen' and 'A century later' explore different types of inequality. Femi explores discrimination by the police force, 'he will see you powerless – plump', when an innocent boy is suspected of a crime based on his racial appearance. The adjective 'powerless' conveys the various power imbalances between the young Black citizen and the older White police officers. It describes how the officers see the boy but also the way he – desperate to convince them of his innocence – hopes to be seen. The disturbing tone is heightened by the adjective 'plump', implying that the officers view this vulnerable teenager as prey to be hunted. By using the modal verb 'will', the poet asserts that this inequality is something that Black people will definitely encounter, which is reinforced through the use of the second person to present his own experience as something universal. In comparison, Dharker's poem focuses on gender inequality and draws on the story of Malala Yousafzai. She creates a more triumphant tone than Femi when stating that 'This girl has won / the right to be ordinary', although the contrast between the verb 'won' and the adjective 'ordinary' highlights that being treated equally should not seem like a special prize. This is emphasised by the noun phrase 'the right', reminding the reader that people should not have to fight for equality.

Questions

QUICK TEST
1. What is the effect of repeating the modal verb 'will' in the poem?
2. How did the police officer seem when he visited the primary school?
3. How does the boy try to appear in front of the police officers?
4. What aspect of British society is being criticised by the poet?

EXAM PRACTICE
Using one or two of the highlighted quotations to learn, write a paragraph exploring how Femi presents fear.

Comparison: Comparing Poetry

How do I prepare for a comparison of two poems?

It is vital that you specifically compare two poems in your exam answer. You will have one poem in front of you (the one named by the examiner in the question) and will need to pick a suitable poem for comparison from your memory of the other 'Worlds and Lives' poems. The exam paper features a list of all the poem titles to help you remember.

It should be easier to find different ideas about the poem that is printed in the paper than from the one you've chosen from memory. For this reason, it is a good idea to start by focusing on the poem from your memory and then link it to the poem you've been given, rather than the other way round.

In the exam, you need to come up with a quick plan. If you have plenty of revision time, practise planning and writing some poetry essays. Take your time getting used to planning so, by the time it comes to the actual exam, you can do it quickly.

Begin by noting down the quotations that you've learned and your thinking about how you can relate them to the exam question. What are the key ideas and the key features in each quotation? You should also consider whether the title is relevant to the question as this gives you additional language to analyse.

For example:

> Compare how poets present the natural world in 'A Portable Paradise' and one other poem.
>
> - 'Lines Written in Early Spring'
>
>   Nature as a source of inspiration; symbolism of spring; contextual link to Romantic movement
>
> - 'I heard a thousand blended notes, / While in a grove I sate reclined'
>
>   Nature is harmonious and relaxing; hyperbole, senses, verb phrase 'sate reclined'
>
> - 'And much it grieved my heart to think / What man has made of man'
>
>   Nature is a contrast to humankind which is full of conflict; contrast with previous lines, metaphor, contextual link to Industrial Revolution
>
> - 'The birds around me hopped and played, / Their thoughts I cannot measure'
>
>   Nature is innocent and happy but very complex; verbs 'hopped and played' and 'cannot measure'
>
> - 'If this belief from heaven be sent, / If such be Nature's holy plan'
>
>   Nature is God's perfect creation; biblical language, personification, link noun 'plan' to the poem's form

Once you've gathered your ideas about your chosen poem, decide what links you can make with the poem named by the examiner. Add to your previous notes. If it helps, you could use a table as this may be useful for clarifying comparisons and contrasts. For example:

Lines Written in Early Spring	A Portable Paradise
1. 'Lines Written in Early Spring' Nature as a source of inspiration; symbolism of spring; contextual link to Romantic movement	1. 'A Portable Paradise' Nature as a source of comfort; extended metaphor
2. 'I heard a thousand blended notes, / While in a grove I sate reclined' Nature is harmonious and relaxing; hyperbole, senses, verb phrase 'sate reclined'	2. 'carry it always / on my person, concealed … / trace its ridges in your pocket, / smell its piney scent on your handkerchief' Nature is precious and relaxing; extended metaphor, senses, imperatives, contextual link to writing in the second person
3. 'And much it grieved my heart to think / What man has made of man' Nature is a contrast to humankind which is full of conflict; contrast with previous lines, metaphor, contextual link to Industrial Revolution	3. 'if your stresses are sustained and daily' The natural world is a contrast to the urban world; noun 'stresses', adjectives 'sustained and daily', contextual link to the autobiographical nature of the poem and the challenges of being an immigrant
4. 'The birds around me hopped and played, / Their thoughts I cannot measure' Nature is innocent and happy but very complex; verbs 'hopped and played' and 'cannot measure'	4. 'your white sands, green hills and fresh fish' Nature is pure and undamaged; adjectives, tricolon, contextual link to Trinidad
5. 'If this belief from heaven be sent, / If such be Nature's holy plan' Nature is God's perfect creation; biblical language, personification, link noun 'plan' to the poem's form	5. 'Shine the lamp on it like the fresh hope / of morning, and keep staring at it till you sleep.' Nature can be a key part of someone's identity, bringing them optimism and comfort; simile, symbolism, imperative

You should be able to find similar or contrasting ideas in your two poems; these ideas can form sections of comparison. Look at whether your ideas run in a coherent order and, if not, rearrange them. For example, in the table above, number 3 could move after the current number 5 so the ideas about the positive qualities of nature are grouped together.

Ideally, you will have a variety of ideas. However, don't worry if some ideas are similar (as with numbers 2 and 4 above). Use opening words or phrases – such as 'Furthermore…', 'This can also be seen…' and 'Similarly…' – at the start of your paragraphs to suggest this is your way of deliberately developing your point.

While you shouldn't worry about having similar points, you should try to avoid always analysing the same literary features. The examiner wants a range of understanding so if every paragraph of your essay analyses metaphors, they won't be impressed. Try to choose quotations that allow different analysis and, when practising essay writing, highlight on your plan the features you're going to explore to make sure they are different.

How do I structure a poetry comparison?

Always start your essay with a very brief introduction. Make sure you clarify which poem you have chosen to use as comparison and try to make a statement that links to the exam question. For example:

> In 'A Portable Paradise' and 'Lines Written in Early Spring', Robinson and Wordsworth convey the beauty of the natural world and how it is a source of pleasure. While Robinson presents nature as a comforting memory that is linked to his heritage, Wordsworth contrasts it with the destructive behaviour of humankind.

One way of approaching the comparison is to write for 20 minutes about one poem then write for 20 minutes about your second poem. However, you must make sure that, when you write about the second poem, you keep linking your ideas back to the first. You can do this using simple opening phrases like: 'In comparison to 'A Portable Paradise'...', 'Like Robinson...', 'Wordsworth displays a similar idea to Robinson when...' and 'Unlike 'A Portable Paradise'...'.

A much better way to write your essay is to keep alternating between the two poems:

Come up with a topic sentence that establishes a point of comparison about the two poems.
Focus on your first poem by clarifying your idea and embedding a quotation.
Analyse how the language of your quotation shows the idea that you have presented. It is better to begin by focusing on language (rather than sentence structures, form or **phonology**) as it is primarily words that convey meaning.
Develop your analysis by considering how the language is emphasised by any effects of sentence structure, form or phonology. At this point, you should also consider whether any of the poem's contexts are relevant to the idea you are presenting.
Using a connective of contrast or comparison (you can start a new paragraph if you wish), introduce your second poem and embed a quotation.
Analyse your second poem in the same way as your first, starting with language and then considering whether any aspects of sentence structure, form, phonology or context could be emphasising the meaning. If you are analysing similar features to your first quotation, make sure you highlight the fact to the examiner as this displays a higher level of comparison.
Starting a new paragraph, come up with a new topic sentence about both poems and repeat the process...

If you're feeling particularly confident in your skills of comparison and analysis, you can try to base your topic sentence round a specific poetic technique. For example: Robinson and Wordsworth both use different senses to convey the comfort that they derive from the natural world. This is difficult to sustain for an entire essay so you may just include one or two sections of comparison that have this specific focus on a poetic technique.

What does a good section of comparison look like?

If you look back at each of the 'Worlds and Lives' poems on pages 4–67, there is a sample section of analysis to help get you thinking about how to compare each poem.

You should try to write fairly equally about the two poems but don't worry about counting up words and making sure it's exact! Try to write in an unhurried and methodical way so you remember to include all the different elements that you need in each section of comparison.

Look at the section of analysis below and annotate it to show how it uses the flow diagram of comparison from page 70.

> 'A Portable Paradise' and 'Lines Written in Early Spring' convey the calming beauty of the natural world. Robinson uses the extended metaphor 'carry it always / on my person, concealed … / trace its ridges in your pocket, / smell its piney scent' to present how his memories of nature are relaxing and precious. The use of the senses in 'trace' and 'smell' suggest the natural world has left a strong impression on him that still brings comfort and pleasure. The adjective 'concealed' and the adverb 'always' emphasise how important this is to him. Much of the poem is written in the second person, using the voice of Robinson's grandmother, and this creates a sense of intimacy that matches the idea of his memories of nature being precious.
>
> Wordsworth also uses the senses to present how the beauty of the natural world comes from its harmony – 'I heard a thousand blended notes, / While in a grove I sate reclined'. The hyperbole suggests that every part of nature exists peacefully together. Like Robinson, he emphasises his pleasure through a suggestion of privacy by using 'grove' to imply peaceful seclusion. This is highlighted by the verb phrase 'sate reclined', suggesting that the natural world is calming and that he feels part of its harmoniousness.

Questions

QUICK TEST
1. Are you allowed to refer to the title of the poem as part of your analysis?
2. Is it better to write one half of your essay on one poem and one half on the other poem, or to alternate your paragraphs between the two poems?
3. What is the point of a topic sentence?
4. In each of your paragraphs, what aspect of the poet's writing is it better to analyse first?

EXAM PRACTICE
Looking at the table on page 69, the flow diagram on page 70 and the exemplar above, write another section of analysis comparing how the poets present the natural world in 'A Portable Paradise' and 'Lines Written in Early Spring'.

Comparing Poetry

Comparison Grid

	Lines Written in Early Spring	England in 1819	Shall earth no more inspire thee	In a London Drawingroom	On an Afternoon Train…	Name Journeys	pot	A Wider View	Homing	A century later	The Jewellery Maker	With Birds You're Never Lonely	A Portable Paradise	Like an Heiress	Thirteen
The natural world	■		■									■	■		
The urban world and pollution				■			■								
Connections with places	■	■	■	■	■	■		■	■	■	■	■	■	■	■
Connections between people		■				■	■	■	■	■	■	■		■	
Heritage and identity					■	■	■	■	■	■	■	■		■	■
Immigration						■			■				■		
Humankind: conflict, oppression, destruction	■	■								■				■	■
Personal struggles			■							■	■	■			■
Inequality		■							■			■			■
Hopes and fears								■			■	■		■	

Comparison — Practice Questions

1. Compare how poets present human nature in 'Lines Written in Early Spring' and one other poem.

Notes

'Lines Written in Early Spring'
- lack of harmony in human nature (compared to singing birds)
- humankind doesn't appreciate what it has (compared to flowers)
- humankind has lost touch with God and nature

'Shall earth no more inspire thee'
- humankind often feels unhappy and directionless
- dissatisfaction is typical of human nature
- humankind has lost touch with nature

The importance of nature to Romantic poets; their views on the Industrial Revolution and the increasing separation between country and urban life; lyric poem compared to dramatic monologue.

2. Compare the ways poets present criticisms of other people in 'England in 1819' and one other poem.

Notes

3. Compare the ways poets use natural imagery in 'Shall earth no more inspire thee' and one other poem.

Notes

4. Compare the ways poets present attitudes towards a place in 'In a London Drawingroom' and one other poem.

Notes

5. Compare the ways poets explore people meeting in 'On an Afternoon Train from Purley to Victoria, 1955' and one other poem.

Notes

6. Compare the ways poets present the experience of immigration in 'Name Journeys' and one other poem.

Notes

7. Compare the ways poets present attitudes towards heritage in 'pot' and one other poem.

Notes

8. Compare the ways poets explore past lives in 'A Wider View' and one other poem.

Notes

9. Compare the ways poets present the importance of identity in 'Homing' and one other poem.

Notes

10. Compare the ways poets present determination in 'A century later' and one other poem.

> **Notes**

11. Compare the ways poets explore the lives of working people in 'The Jewellery Maker' and one other poem.

> **Notes**

12. Compare the ways poets present connections with people and places in 'With Birds You're Never Lonely' and one other poem.

> **Notes**

13. Compare the ways poets use extended metaphor in 'A Portable Paradise' and one other poem.

Notes

14. Compare the ways poets explore humankind's relationship with nature in 'Like an Heiress' and one other poem.

Notes

15. Compare the ways poets present injustice in 'Thirteen' and one other poem.

Notes

The Exam: Tips and Assessment Objectives

Quick tips

- You will get one question on the 'Worlds and Lives' poems (plus questions on the other two collections that can be studied: 'Love and Relationships' and 'Power and Conflict').
- The examiner will name one poem and it will be printed for you. Read it carefully to fully refresh your memory. You will need to think of a second poem from the 'Worlds and Lives' collection that is suitable for comparison.
- Make sure you know what the question is asking you and underline the key words.
- You should spend about 45 minutes on your poetry comparison response. Allow yourself five minutes to plan your answer so there is some structure to your essay.
- Try to begin your essay with a clear statement, or thesis, that establishes your overall response to the exam question. This will give your essay a clearer focus and help you to fully explore the two poems.
- All your paragraphs should contain a clear idea, a relevant reference to a poem (ideally a quotation) and analysis of how the poet conveys this idea. Your paragraphs should be linked through comparison and, when relevant, you should link your comments to the poems' contexts.
- It can sometimes help, after each paragraph, to quickly re-read the question to keep yourself focused on the exam task.
- Keep your writing concise. If you waste time 'waffling', you won't be able to include the full range of analysis and understanding that the mark scheme requires.
- It is a good idea to remember what the mark scheme is asking of you.

AO1: Understand and compare the poems (12 marks)

This is all about coming up with a range of points that match the question, supporting your ideas with references from the poems, and writing your essay in a mature, academic style.

Lower	Middle	Upper
The essay has some good comparative ideas that are mostly relevant. Some quotations and references are used to support the ideas.	A clear essay that always focuses on the exam question. Quotations and references support ideas effectively. The response includes several comparisons.	A convincing, well-structured essay that answers the question fully. Quotations and references are well-chosen and integrated into sentences. The response provides a detailed and thoughtful comparison of the two poems.

AO2: Analyse effects of the poets' language, structure and form (12 marks)

You need to comment on how specific words, language techniques or sentence structures and the poetic form or metre allow the poets to get their ideas across. To achieve this, you will need to have learned good quotations to analyse.

Lower	Middle	Upper
Identification of some different methods used by the poets to convey meaning. Some subject terminology.	Explanation of the poets' different methods. Clear understanding of the effects of these methods. Accurate use of subject terminology.	Analysis of the full range of the poets' methods. Thorough exploration of the effects of these methods. Accurate range of subject terminology.

AO3: Understand the relationship between the poems and their contexts (6 marks)

For this part of the mark scheme, you need to show your understanding of how the meaning of the poems has been affected by the ways in which they have been written. You could also consider how the meaning of the poems is affected by who wrote them and when they were written.

Lower	Middle	Upper
Some awareness of how ideas are affected by the poems' contexts.	References to relevant aspects of context show a clear understanding.	Exploration is linked to specific aspects of the poems' contexts to show a detailed understanding.

Planning a Poetry Response

How might the exam question be phrased?
A typical poetry comparison question will read like this:

> Compare how poets present oppression in 'England in 1819' and one other poem. [30 marks]

How do I work out what to do?
The focus of this question is clear: the presentation of oppression.

'Compare' and 'how' are important elements of this question.

For AO1, 'compare' shows that you need to make a series of structured and well-developed comparisons about oppression in the poems. The examiner names one poem and you have to choose a second that is suitable for comparison. Only the poem named in the question will be printed for you; ideally, you should include quotations that you have learned from the other poem but, if necessary, you can make a clear reference to a specific part of the poem.

For AO2, 'how' makes it clear that you need to analyse the different ways in which the poets use language, structure and form to help to show things about oppression.

You also need to remember to link your comments to the poems' contexts to achieve your AO3 marks. Think about the way the poems have been written and how this has affected the ways in which meaning is conveyed.

How can I plan my essay?
You have approximately 45 minutes to write your essay.

This isn't long but you should spend the first five minutes writing a quick plan. This will help you to focus your thoughts and produce a well-structured comparative essay.

Try to come up with a clear thesis statement that gives an overview of your response to the question, plus three or four comparisons (they can be similarities and/or differences). Each of these comparisons can then be written up as a paragraph. For more detailed advice on planning a comparison, look back at pages 68–71.

You can plan in whatever way you find most useful. Some students like to just make a quick list of points and then re-number them into a logical order. Spider diagrams are particularly popular; look at the example on the next page.

'England in 1819'

Oppression = inequality caused by legal system

'Golden and sanguine laws which tempt and slay'

Oppression = violence

'A people starved and stabbed in th' untilled field'

* context – Peterloo Massacre; subversion of sonnet form

Oppression = need for revolution

'a glorious Phantom may / Burst, to illumine our tempestuous day'

* context – Peterloo Massacre; less definite about the possibility of change

'A century later'

Oppression = legal and social inequality in female education

'The school-bell is a call to battle, / every step to class, a step into the firing-line'

* context – Malala Yousafzai; different 'rights' compared with the lives of most readers.

Oppression = violence

'Surrendered, surrounded, she / takes the bullet in the head / and walks on'

* context – although based on a real event, lack of specificity and use of third person make this about widespread oppression

Oppression = need for revolution

'A murmur, a swarm. Behind her, one by one, / the schoolgirls are standing up'

* context – related to worldwide outcry over Malala's shooting; more positive and definite.

Presentation of oppression

Summary

- Make sure you know what the focus of the essay is.
- Remember to compare the two poems.
- Remember to analyse how ideas are conveyed by each poet.
- Try to relate your ideas to the poems' contexts.

Questions

QUICK TEST
1. What key skills do you need to show in your answer?
2. What are the benefits of quickly planning your essay?
3. Why is it better to have learned quotations for the exam?

EXAM PRACTICE
Plan a response to the follow exam question:
Compare how poets present feelings about a place in 'Like an Heiress' and one other poem.
[30 marks]

The Exam
Grade 5 Annotated Response

Compare how poets present oppression in 'England in 1819' and one other poem. [30 marks]

'England in 1819' and 'A century later' both explore oppression. The two poets show that people are unequal, are violently oppressed and need a revolution. [1]

Both poems present groups of people being oppressed through inequality. Shelley describes how unfair the legal system is because it says it serves everyone but actually does people harm. 'Golden and sanguine laws which tempt and slay'. This is a metaphor. The word 'golden' makes the legal system sound perfect but the word 'tempt' means it's actually dangerous, it is only pretending to be a fair and equal system for all. This can also be seen in the violent word 'slay' which emphasises how bad the legal system is by suggesting it causes people's deaths. [2]

Similarly, Dharker criticises society for its legal and social inequality because she writes about Malala Yousafzai and how women suffer from inequality. [3] The poem has a frightening tone because there are images of schooling that are matched with descriptions of war, showing how Malala had to fight for her education. She describes how people get shot for going to school. This is a frightening example of oppression because it means that people who speak out against inequality or try to take action are killed. [4]

Both poems present groups of people being oppressed through violence. Shelley describes the Peterloo Massacre, 'A people starved and stabbed in th' untilled field'. The verb 'stabbed' shows oppression because the government is murdering people who protest against it. The words 'stabbed' and 'starved' are alliteration. The word 'starved' is also about inequality because it means that the people are hungry unlike the rich people who would have had lots of food and led comfortable lives. It's also clear they are poor because they work in fields. [5]

Similarly, Dharker describes Malala being violently oppressed. 'Surrendered, surrounded'. She uses adjectives to make her sound vulnerable which makes the reader feel sorry for her. 'Surrounded' suggests that she is outnumbered while 'surrendered' sounds like she has received no support and people have handed her over to the authorities to be oppressed. There's some alliteration again. [6] She also describes Malala getting shot but Dharker is a bit more positive than Shelley because of her enjambment. This is when a sentence of poetry continues across the next line without pausing. In the poem, Malala cannot be stopped because she is calm and the bullet didn't kill her so she is standing up to oppression. [7]

Both poems present groups of people standing up to oppression and being revolutionary. Shelley describes all the people who have been oppressed coming out of their graves and overthrowing the government. 'graves from which a glorious Phantom may / Burst, to illumine our tempestuous day'. Shelley uses contrasts because 'tempestuous' shows how frightening and oppressive England is whereas 'glorious' shows it could be great. Shelley is saying that revolution would make England a better place. [8]

Similarly, Dharker describes Malala getting everyone together to protest about women not having equal access to education. This is oppressive because they will never get good jobs or think for themselves. She compares the women to bees which is a metaphor. 'A murmur, a swarm. Behind her, one by one, / the schoolgirls are standing up'. The description of the girls standing up shows that they are demanding their right to an education. 'Behind her' means that Malala is leading them so they don't feel oppressed anymore but they are still being brave because they are only schoolgirls. [9]

1. Clear introduction showing which other poem is being used for comparison. The student could identify how the poems are different in order to establish an argument or exploration. AO1
2. Clear point, evidence and analysis. However, the quotation could be embedded, the expression considered more and subject terminology used more effectively. AO2
3. A connective is used to clarify comparison. There is a link to context but this could be more subtle. AO1/AO3
4. There is some good explanation of the second poem. However, the lack of a quotation means that the writing is more descriptive than analytical. AO1/AO2
5. This is a good attempt to develop the essay, although the topic sentence needs varying from the one used in the second paragraph. There is some secure analysis and a clear link to context. However, there is some feature-spotting and ideas could be more concise and precise. AO1/AO2/AO3
6. Despite some feature-spotting, there is some good analysis of language. AO2
7. This is a good attempt to develop comparison and analyse form but ideas could be conveyed more precisely. AO1/AO2
8. Analysis is good but it could be more technical and developed further. The quotation needs embedding. AO1/AO2
9. There is a clear comparison but some feature-spotting and a tendency to describe rather than analyse. The student has not ended with a conclusion. AO1/AO2

Questions

EXAM PRACTICE

Choose a paragraph of this essay. Read it through a few times then try to rewrite and improve it. You might:

- improve the sophistication of the language or the clarity of expression
- replace a reference with a quotation or use a better quotation
- ensure quotations are embedded in the sentence
- provide more detailed, or a wider range of, analysis
- use subject terminology more effectively
- link some context to the analysis more effectively.

The Exam: Grade 7+ Annotated Response

A proportion of the best top-band answers will be awarded Grade 8 or Grade 9. To achieve this, you should aim for a sophisticated, fluid and nuanced response that displays flair and originality.

> Compare how poets present oppression in 'England in 1819' and one other poem. [30 marks]

'England in 1819' and 'A century later' both explore how oppression is achieved through inequality and violence. However, while Shelley hopes for change, Dharker presents a more positive view that oppression ultimately fails. [1]

Both poems present people being oppressed through inequality. Shelley's metaphor, 'Golden and sanguine laws which tempt and slay', uses verbs and colours to suggest the legal system appears to serve everybody but, in reality, harms the average citizen. While 'golden' symbolises perfection, 'tempt' is more **equivocal**, suggesting something aspirational yet dangerous or **duplicitous**. Similarly, 'sanguine' can mean optimistic but also has connotations of blood which matches the violence of 'slay'. This could link to the poem's leech imagery of a 'fainting country' where the population has been exploited and weakened by its rulers. [2]

Drawing on the experiences of Malala Yousafzai [3], Dharker offers a similar exploration of legal and social inequality but focuses on its impact on women. Like Shelley, she uses a metaphor [4], 'The school-bell is a call to battle, / every step to class, a step into the firing-line', to present how individual rights are in danger. The juxtaposition of images relating to school and war emphasises how things that some readers may take for granted need to be fought for in other countries [5]. She creates a similarly frightening tone to 'England in 1819', particularly the image of the 'firing-line' which indicates that people who speak out are killed.

Violence as a tool of oppression is a motif in both poems. Shelley's description of 'A people starved and stabbed in th' untilled field' refers to the Peterloo Massacre. The verb 'stabbed' depicts the state as murderous and silencing any protests. The alliteration with 'starved' also highlights the vulnerability of the victims. This is emphasised by 'prey', implying they are seen as animals and accusing the army of 'liberticide' which indicates that freedom is being eradicated. His use of the sonnet form could be relevant here, subverting its traditional associations to indicate his hatred of oppression; however, it could also be seen as representing his love for his fellow people. [6]

Dharker conveys similar oppression when she depicts the schoolgirl as 'Surrendered, surrounded, she / takes the bullet in the head' to highlight the vulnerability of the victim. 'Surrounded' suggests she is outnumbered while 'surrendered' could imply she has received no support; as with 'England in 1819', alliteration links these two words to emphasise her lack of power. By writing in the third person and only alluding to, not specifying, real events, both authors indicate that oppression is widespread and affects different people. However, while Dharker presents the brutality of the shooting, her enjambment of 'and walks on' suggests defiance as the girl cannot be stopped. [7]

Ultimately, both poets call for revolution to end oppression. Shelley's vision is more fantastical, using the image of 'graves from which a glorious Phantom may / Burst, to illumine our tempestuous day' to suggest people will rise up in remembrance of the Peterloo Massacre's victims. The contrasting adjectives 'tempestuous' and 'glorious' convey how revolution could remove the horrors of the oppressive state and make England a better place. Shelley emphasises this by using light to symbolise hope. In comparison, Dharker depicts the outcry that stemmed from the attempted murder. Her images of 'A murmur, a swarm. Behind her, one by one, / the schoolgirls are standing up' convey growing anger and support for female equality. Whereas Shelley used the modal verb 'may' to suggest the possibility of change, Dharker's 'are' is much more definite and this is highlighted by the more positive description of living schoolgirls demanding their rights. [8]

1. Clear introduction, establishing a sense of comparison and argument. AO1
2. Embedded quotations and sophisticated analysis of language, including awareness of alternative meanings. A range of terminology is applied accurately. AO2
3. Good use of context, developed through the paragraph and firmly linked to the surrounding analysis. AO3
4. Clear comparison of theme and poetic devices. AO1/AO2
5. Context is linked to analysis of structure. AO2/AO3
6. Successful development of argument through sophisticated language choices and sustained analysis of language and form. AO1/AO2
7. Exploratory analysis and comparison, strengthened by considering context and exploring the effects of form. AO1/AO2/AO3
8. Good conclusion, highlighted through close comparison of language and consideration of context. AO1/AO2/AO3

Questions

EXAM PRACTICE

Spend 45 minutes writing an answer to the following question:
Compare how poets present feelings about a place in 'Like an Heiress' and one other poem. [30 marks]
Remember to use the plan you have already prepared.

Glossary

Glossary of literary terms

Adjective – a word that describes a noun

Adverb – a word that describes a verb

Alliteration – a series of words beginning with the same sound

Allusion – a reference to something without specifically stating it

Anaphora – repeating words or phrases in a structured way (such as at the start of stanzas)

Atmosphere – the overall tone or mood of a piece of writing

Caesura – a pause within a line of poetry, created by a punctuation mark

Colloquial – everyday, informal language

Conjunction – a word used to connect two clauses, such as 'and', 'but', 'while'

Consonance – a series of words containing the same consonant sounds

Couplet – two lines of poetry

Determiner – a word that clarifies a noun, such as 'the', 'my', 'this'

Dialogue – speech

Direct address – speaking directly to the listener or reader

Dramatic monologue – a poem in which the poet adopts the voice, or persona, of a character and addresses an imagined audience

Duologue – dialogue between two people

End-stopped – using punctuation (such as a comma, full stop or dash) at the end of a line of poetry

Enjambment – continuing a sentence across lines of poetry without end-stopping

Euphemism – replacing a harsh or taboo word or phrase with a milder, more indirect one

Extended metaphor – a metaphor that is continued throughout a series of images

First person – using I (singular) or we (plural) to show a personal or shared experience

Foreshadowing – suggesting something that is going to happen later

Free verse – a poem that uses neither a specific metre nor a set rhyme scheme

Ghazal – a form of Indian poetry, often exploring spiritual love or the pain of loss

Half-rhyme – a near rhyme, needing one vowel sound to change to achieve a full rhyme

Hyperbole – exaggerated language

Imperative – a sentence or word that contains an order

Intensifier – a type of adverb used to add emphasis or force

Irony – saying one thing in order to deliberately suggest the opposite; a situation that appears deliberately the opposite of what you might expect

Juxtaposition – placing two things next to each other, usually to create a contrast

Lyric poetry – a formal poem, expressing personal feelings and emotions

Metaphor – a descriptive technique, using comparison to say one thing is something else

Metonymy – referring to something by using the name of something else (such as an object or quality) that is closely related to it

Modal verb – a verb showing the necessity or possibility of another verb (such as *could* eat, *should* eat, *might* eat)

Mood – the dominant emotion or atmosphere of a piece of writing

Motif – a recurring idea in a piece of literature

Noun – a naming word for a person, place, animal or object

Noun phrase – a series of words that functions like a noun

Pathos – a mood of pity or sadness

Personification – describing an object or idea as if it has human characteristics

Phonology – sounds within speech

Plosives – harsh sounds formed through a sudden release of air from the mouth

Preposition – a word that shows time, location or direction, such as 'at', 'on', 'to'

Pronoun – a word used as a substitute for a noun; personal pronouns show who is speaking (I, he, she, they); possessive pronouns indicate ownership (my, her, their); singular and plural pronouns indicate whether one or more person is involved (I/they); indefinite pronouns refer to something unspecific (all, everyone, anything)

Proper noun – a name of a person, place, organisation, etc.

Prosaic – language that is more typical of normal communication, rather than sounding poetic

Quatrain – a four-line stanza

Repetition – saying something more than once to achieve a specific effect

Rhetorical question – a question used to make the reader think, rather than to gain an answer

Rhyme – words with the same sound (patterns of rhyme can be noted using letters, so *abab* shows that the first and third lines of a poem rhyme, as do the second and fourth lines)

Second person – writing using the pronoun 'you' (as opposed to first or third person)

Sibilance – repetition of s sounds

Simile – a descriptive technique, using like or as to form a comparison

Sonnet – a fourteen-line poem in iambic pentameter with a fixed rhyme scheme, usually focusing on love

Stanza – a group of lines in a poem (like a paragraph of poetry)

Superlative – describing the most something can be (such as heaviest, smallest)

Symbol – an object or colour used to represent a different meaning

Third person – writing using the pronouns he, she or they (as opposed to first person, I)

Tone – the way words suggest a particular mood or feeling

Tricolon – ideas or words arranged into a pattern of three for a specific effect

Verb – a word that expresses an action or state of being

Verb phrase – a series of words that functions like a verb

Volta – a change or 'turn' of ideas or emotions in a sonnet

Vowel sounds – the sounds created when pronouncing vowels; these can be short (a, e, i, o, u) or long (A, E, I, O, U, OO, AH)

Metre

Metre – the rhythmic structure of a line of poetry, based on patterns of stress, created through the type and number of metrical feet it contains. If a line uses two feet, it is dimeter, three feet is trimeter, four feet is tetrameter, five feet is pentameter, etc.

Iamb – this is the most regularly used metrical foot; it consists of an unstressed beat followed by a stressed beat

Iambic trimeter – a line consisting of three iambs

Iambic tetrameter – a line consisting of four iambs

Iambic pentameter – a line consisting of five iambs

General glossary

Abstract – existing as a thought rather than being a physical object

Addressee – the person being spoken to or written to

Advocate – to openly support or recommend something

Alignment – a position of agreement and evenness

Anecdotal – based on stories of personal experiences

Arrogance – thinking that you are better or more important than others

Artefact – an object of cultural or historical significance

Assimilation – the process through which those of a different heritage gain the basic habits, attitudes and mode of life of a different culture

Asynchronous – not existing at the same time

Aural – relating to the ear or hearing

Autobiographical – about the writer's own life

Barista – a person who prepares and serves coffee

Bower – a shaded area under trees in a wood or garden

Brotherhood – people linked by a common interest

Chastened – punished or made to feel in the wrong

Cholera – an infectious disease

Colonialism – taking control of a country in order to exploit its people and resources

Comrade – a fellow soldier or colleague

Conformity – behaving the same as everyone else

Conical – shaped like a cone

Corrupt – being dishonest, usually for monetary gain

Deft – neatly and quickly skilful

Degeneration – getting worse; declining

Deities – gods or goddesses

Despondency – hopelessness; unhappiness

Dialect – words that are specific to a region (such as Cockney rhyming slang)

Diaspora – people who have spread from their homeland to other countries

Discrimination – unfair treatment due to a specific characteristic, such as race, gender or age

Discordant – a harsh sound due to a lack of harmony; disagreeing

Disillusionment – disappointment upon finding that something isn't as good as expected

Dregs – the leftovers or most worthless part of something

Dual heritage – having two ethnic or cultural backgrounds

Duplicitous – deliberately misleading; untrustworthy

Dynasties – a succession of people from the same ruling family

Elocution – the skill of clear and "correct" pronunciation

Empathy – the ability to understand another's feelings

Empire – a number of countries ruled over by one state or monarch

Equivocal – open to more than one interpretation; uncertain and ambiguous

Ethical – relating to moral principles

Establishment – the elements of society that exercise power and control

Exploitation – treating people unequally for personal financial gain

Fate – something that is predetermined or bound to happen; something's outcome or the end of someone's life

Ferrous – containing iron

Forge – to shape a metal object by heating it in a furnace and hammering it; a blacksmith's workshop

Futile – pointless; bound to fail

Grove – a small wood

Guttural – describing harsh sounds produced in the throat

Heiress – a woman who inherits something

Hemp – thick fibres for weaving into sacks

Heritage – valued objects or qualities passed down by previous generations

Heteronormativity – the assumption that "normal" relationships exist only between a man and a woman and that anything outside of this is "abnormal"

Hovel – a simple and unpleasant dwelling

Hypocrisy – pretending to have high standards while behaving otherwise

Idealism – an unrealistically perfect view of something

Idolatry – worship of idols; extreme admiration or love

Ignorant – lacking knowledge or awareness; rude

Illumine – light up; illuminate

Industrial Revolution – the period, from 1760 to around 1830, when Britain changed to mechanised manufacturing processes

Inequality – a lack of equality; unfairness

Inevitable – unavoidable; something that will definitely happen

Infertile – unable to grow vegetation; unable to have children

Insincere – not expressing genuine feelings

Instigator – the person who starts something (such as a conversation or a project)

Insurmountable – too great to overcome

Lament – to express grief about something

Marginalised – someone or something that is not seen as important or of equal significance and is relegated to the edge of society and excluded from full participation in life

Monarchy – the royal family

Monotony – a boring lack of variety

Neuro-diverse – when someone's brain processes, learns or behaves differently from what is considered typical

Non-standard English – a version of English that isn't grammatically "correct" or that contains a lot of slang

Notorious – being well known for something bad

Ominous – threatening

Omniscient – knowing and seeing everything

Oppression – treating people harshly in order to control them

Optimism – having a hopeful, positive outlook

Patois – a dialect or non-standard form of speech

Patriarchy – a system in which men hold power

Perception – viewpoint

Pessimism – having a negative outlook that expects the worst

Phantom – ghost

Philosophical – thinking about the nature of existence and reality

Pine – to long for something

Profound – deeply felt

Punjabi – a language spoken mainly in north-western India and eastern Pakistan

Queer – not corresponding to traditional or typical ideas of sexuality or gender

Rebound – bounce back

Received pronunciation – the standard, or "correct", way to pronounce words

Reclined – leaning or laying back in a relaxed position

Regal – of, relating to or suitable for royalty

Resilience – the toughness to keep going despite difficult challenges

Repatriation – to return something, or someone, to its original homeland

Revolution – overthrowing a social order or government and replacing it with a new system

Romanticism – a literary and artistic movement from the late 1700s to the mid-1800s, focusing on feelings, ideals and the importance of nature

Roving – constantly moving

Rural – relating to the countryside

Sanguine – blood-red; optimistic despite a bad situation

Scorn – intense disapproval or dislike

Senate – a group of people with legal powers

Simultaneously – at the same time

Slay – kill

Social realism – a realistic image of life in order to make a comment on society or politics

Statute – a law

Subvert – to overturn expectations or conventions; to undermine and corrupt

Suppress – to prevent the expression or development of something

Swathe – to wrap in layers of fabric

Systemic racism – when long-term racism has led to it becoming an established (but not openly admitted) part of an organisation or system; also known as institutional racism

Temperament – a person's nature

Tempestuous – stormy; full of conflict

Tyrant – a cruel, oppressive ruler

Uniformity – everything being the same

Unrepealed – remaining in force

Urban – relating to towns or cities

Victorian – the period of British history relating to the reign of Queen Victoria (1837–1901)

Wayward – difficult to control; unpredictable

Wield – hold and use something (such as a weapon or influence)

Wilderness – a barren region where it is difficult to survive

Workhouse – a public institution where the poor were forced to live, being given food and lodging in return for work

Wreath – a circular arrangement of flowers and/or leaves for decoration or laying on a grave; a curl of smoke

Glossary

Answers

Pages 4–7: Lines Written in Early Spring
QUICK TEST
1. Nature is harmonious while humankind is always in conflict.
2. He is unhappy: 'sad thoughts', 'grieved my heart', 'lament'.
3. The simplicity could suggest the innocence and purity of nature.
4. Rhetorical question

EXAM PRACTICE
Ideas might include how images of harmony and calm ('blended notes … sate reclined') suggest nature relaxes the speaker; nature makes the speaker happy (verbs like 'hopped and played') but he's also in awe of, or curious about, it ('thoughts I cannot measure'); religious imagery suggests he feels nature is a thing of perfection ('from heaven') that we should take inspiration from when living our lives ('holy plan').

Pages 8–11: England in 1819
QUICK TEST
1. Unpopular, aged and incapable: 'old, mad, blind, despised, and dying'.
2. It ignores public opinion; is unintelligent and inbred; is ignorant about others' struggles; doesn't care about the country and exploits its people.
3. The army, the legal establishment, the Church and the Government.
4. Revolution

EXAM PRACTICE
Ideas might include how the opening list of adjectives presents England as run by someone who is incapable and unpopular; the 'leech' simile presents England as being exploited by rulers who are unsympathetic and ignorant of the people's struggles; personification is used to suggest that the legal establishment only works to punish English citizens ('tempt and slay'); metonymy ('a book sealed') implies the Church keeps people ignorant of the true meaning of Christianity; the country is in a state of chaos (the adjective 'tempestuous').

Pages 12–15: Shall earth no more inspire thee
QUICK TEST
1. The person is unhappy, possibly due to a lack of inspiration.
2. The speaker appears to be a personification of nature.
3. The speaker offers comfort; this could be seen as inspiration ('enchant'), relaxation ('soothe') or happiness ('my sunshine pleases').
4. It has uniformity due to the regular *abab* rhyme scheme and the iambic rhythm.

EXAM PRACTICE
Ideas might include how nature is personified as something relaxing ('my mountain breezes … soothe') and inspiring ('enchant'); use of **anaphora** ('I know'), and metaphor ('drive thy griefs away') suggest nature is confident in its ability to heal humankind; the imperative 'Return and dwell with me' is a persuasive offer of safety or comfort.

Pages 16–19: In a London Drawingroom
QUICK TEST
1. A long row of houses.
2. A wall of fog.
3. They appear unhappy and discontented.
4. Stressful

EXAM PRACTICE
Ideas might include how London is depressing and oppressive (the simile 'like solid fog') and how the urban development is damaging nature (the metaphor 'cutting the sky'); images of darkness symbolise unhappiness and illustrate the problem of overdevelopment, such as the simile 'as in ways o'erhung / By thickest canvass' and the metaphor 'golden rays / Are clothed in hemp'; the verb phrases 'hurry on' and 'look upon the ground' suggest that people are unhappy and too busy with their lives to worry about others; the metaphor 'one huge prison-house & court' indicates that everyone is trapped in an unhappy life, constantly feeling judged by others and in danger of being sent to the workhouse.

Pages 20–23: On an Afternoon Train from Purley to Victoria, 1955

QUICK TEST

1. He is startled or surprised.
2. He replies very briefly, merely copying her words.
3. He sees 'empty city streets lit dimly' at dawn and his 'father's big banana field' in darkness.
4. She presumes he wasn't born in England and thinks Jamaica is part of Africa.

EXAM PRACTICE

Ideas might include how the image of 'empty city streets lit dimly' could symbolise the speaker's loneliness in London; however, when he thinks of his father's farm, the 'darkness' could symbolise how he wasn't happy or fulfilled there either; the juxtaposition of these two images could present the struggle of migrating somewhere and belonging in two different places; the woman's dissatisfaction with England could be suggested by her idealised description of Jamaica ('such sunny country'); the speaker's comment that 'Snow falls elsewhere' might imply that people are restless, don't always see the positives of their own country or are always searching for a better place to live.

Pages 24–27: Name Journeys

QUICK TEST

1. Rama, Sita and Draupadi
2. All three faced challenges in life.
3. Struggling to speak English (and losing her original language of Punjabi).
4. They couldn't pronounce her name.

EXAM PRACTICE

Ideas might include the metaphor for losing her original language ('became dislodged') and her culture not being valued ('hit infertile English soil'); the phrase 'my name became a stumble' suggesting people became embarrassed around her because they couldn't pronounce her name, implying also that she became embarrassed by her own cultural identity; the metaphor 'void of history and memory' indicating that she became disconnected from her heritage and felt empty as a result.

Pages 28–33: pot

QUICK TEST

1. A Nigerian pot in a museum.
2. The true story of how it came to England (an act of cultural theft).
3. She wants to smash the glass cabinet and return the pot to its original land.
4. As well as the pot representing cultural theft, it also represents the wider issue of colonialism and its effects; the pot could also be an immigrant or someone with dual heritage; at the end of the poem, the writer also links the pot to prisoners at Guantanamo Bay.

EXAM PRACTICE

Ideas might include how the phrase 'I need you to tell me the rest pot / tell me' uses a modal verb and repetition to suggest that people with dual heritage sometimes do not have access to the history of their non-White heritage, despite it being vital for understanding their own identity; this also appears in the metaphor 'empty pot / growl if you hear me', suggesting that not fully understanding oneself leads to dissatisfaction and anger; the positive language of affection in 'they were happy / to see me / laughed a lot' (contrasting with the earlier line, 'you're not really one of us') conveys how people with dual heritage should not fear the rejection of others and, instead, actively discover the different parts of their identity.

Pages 34–37: A Wider View

QUICK TEST

1. Leeds in 1869
2. He had a difficult life: he had poor living conditions and a tough job at one of the local factories.
3. The Tower Works factory (specifically its chimney).
4. Our present is linked to our past; it helps to shape our identities.

EXAM PRACTICE

Ideas might include how the verb phrase 'searched for spaces' indicates that her great-great-grandfather worked very hard to try to achieve a better life; referring to 'the smoke-filled sky to stack his dreams' suggests that he was living in a polluted area, while the accompanying metaphor might indicate that he felt hopeless at times; the phrase 'craved the comfort' suggests he was desperate to escape his hardships; 'the din of engines, looms and shuttles' uses the noun 'din' and the tricolon of machine parts to convey how the overwhelming noise of machinery made his time at work unpleasant.

Pages 38–41: Homing

QUICK TEST

1. The locked box, representing how the person hid their accent.
2. The Black Country accent
3. They were given elocution lessons at school and punished if they didn't speak "correctly", making them feel ashamed of their accent.
4. The speaker loves the accent, seeing it as something to be proud of and celebrate.

EXAM PRACTICE

Ideas might include how the extended metaphor of the box with its 'lock rusted shut' indicates that the speaker's relative felt ashamed of their accent but was also upset to hide it; the 'hours of elocution' suggests being repeatedly taught to believe that their natural way of speaking was "wrong"; the metaphor 'years of lost words spill out' implies that, by not using their accent or any dialect words, the relative was never fully connected to their identity and did not express their true self.

Pages 42–45: A century later

QUICK TEST

1. An education (or freedom and equal access to education)
2. Ominous, suggesting something bad is going to happen.
3. It becomes more triumphant or defiant.
4. War imagery

EXAM PRACTICE

Ideas might include how the phrase 'every step to class, a step into the firing-line' uses contrasting imagery to turn what for most young people is a normal part of their daily routine into something dangerous and frightening; 'Surrendered, surrounded' has connotations of vulnerability, not being supported by the authorities and being outnumbered; however, 'takes the bullet in the head / and walks on' uses metaphor and enjambment to convey how people can stand up to oppression and defeat it; similarly, '*Bullet, she says, you are stupid. / You have failed*' presents oppression as pathetic, based on ignorance and beatable.

Pages 46–49: The Jewellery Maker

QUICK TEST

1. 'neat as soldiers' suggests he carefully organises his workspace and looks after his tools.
2. The metaphors in lines 10–12 (as well as the natural imagery and verbs within those metaphors).
3. Give his wife a better life (specifically, decorate the house in gold and give her lots of fine clothes and jewellery).
4. Her skin is 'wrinkled by sun' but theirs is 'unlined'; she only has one simple piece of jewellery whereas they will wear his ornate jewellery.

EXAM PRACTICE

Ideas might include how the poet uses contrasting nouns and adjectives to show that the jewellery maker wants to be able to replace his wife's 'simple cotton dress' with 'fine-spun gold'; more contrasts are used to suggest the easier life that wealth brings: his wife's skin 'wrinkled by sun' contrasts with the 'clear-eyed, bird-boned, unlined skin' of those whom he imagines buy his jewellery; his wife's wedding ring, 'her only jewellery a plain gold band, worn thin', also symbolises a life of poverty through the images of simplicity, thinness and being worn down (which also contrasts with the ornate liveliness of the jewellery that he makes for the richer women).

Pages 50–55: With Birds You're Never Lonely

QUICK TEST

1. He 'can't hear the barista' in order to give his order; the background noises are overwhelming.
2. His recent trip to a Zelandia forest.

3. Turn off his hearing aids.
4. He seems 'jealous' of them being unhearing and of their sense of belonging; he is also impressed by their size and strength.

EXAM PRACTICE

Ideas might include how verbs and sibilance are used in 'Spoons slam, steam rises' to convey how background noises can be overwhelming for someone with hearing aids; this is also conveyed by the noise of the birds, 'They landed by my feet, blaring so loudly', with the verb conveying harshness while the intensifier and adverb convey how uncomfortable the sound is for him; the modal verb in 'I had to turn off my hearing aids' makes him seem under attack with no choice but to respond; the idea of being attacked continues through personification, 'The forest spat all the birds back', with the verb 'spat' making the noise sound particularly unwelcome.

Pages 56–59: A Portable Paradise

QUICK TEST

1. His grandmother
2. It will comfort him in times of difficulty or stress.
3. It is an extended metaphor.
4. His youth in Trinidad: 'white sands, green hills and fresh fish'.

EXAM PRACTICE

Ideas might include how the poet uses senses and verbs to convey how memories of a place can bring pleasure and invigoration – 'trace its ridges … smell its piney scent … hum its anthem' – with the tricolon building up these small details to emphasise the impact they can have; the possessive pronoun in 'your paradise' highlights the idea of something personal that is part of one's identity, while 'white sands, green hills and fresh fish' uses images of nature to suggest relaxation and happiness; the simile 'Shine the lamp on it like the fresh hope / of morning' indicates that memories of place bring optimism and help dispel any troubles, while 'keep staring at it till you sleep' returns to the idea of those thoughts bringing relaxation.

Pages 60–63: Like an Heiress

QUICK TEST

1. A sonnet
2. A beach in Guyana (possibly the coastal village where the poet grew up).
3. It is deserted and polluted.
4. The initially happy, proud tone turns to one of disappointment and disillusionment, becoming pessimistic in the final lines.

EXAM PRACTICE

Ideas might include how the poet uses metaphor ('wave of rubbish') to show how nature is being overtaken by pollution; the noun phrases 'car tyres, plastic bottles, styrofoam cups' depict how our daily lives are harming the environment, and the pattern of three builds up these images to emphasise the scale of the pollution; the metaphor 'sun's burning treasury' could be an image of global warming, suggesting the hot weather looks beautiful but is becoming dangerous; this is reinforced by the final line, 'the quickening years and fate of our planet', where the adjective 'quickening' either suggests we are running out of time to save the planet or that its destruction is getting closer (the noun 'fate' has a pessimistic tone, indicating that she fears our planet is doomed).

Pages 64–67: Thirteen

QUICK TEST

1. It suggests the events of the poem 'will' definitely happen to Black people.
2. Positive, optimistic, friendly
3. Friendly, innocent, harmless
4. Systemic racism in the police service

EXAM PRACTICE

Ideas might include how the verb 'cornered' suggests feeling trapped and vulnerable, which is heightened by the adjective 'another' indicating he is outnumbered; the verb 'patted' could sound gentle but, in the context of the officer's systemic racism, has a threatening tone; the verb 'praying' conveys the boy's fear and desperation for help, and this is emphasised by the metaphor 'fear condenses on your lips', indicating that he is nervously sweating but also implying that fear is emanating from him; the adjective 'powerless' conveys the boy's sense of vulnerability and this is reinforced by the adjective 'plump', as if he is the police officers' prey; the metaphor 'the two men cast lots for your organs' suggests his terror that the men are going to kill him for fun.

Pages 68–71: Comparing Poetry

QUICK TEST
1. Yes, the title can provide you with extra language to analyse.
2. Keep alternating between the two poems.
3. It establishes a point of comparison about the poems, showing the examiner that you are meeting the assessment criteria.
4. Start by focusing on language then consider how meaning is emphasised by sentence structure, form or phonology.

EXAM PRACTICE
Use the flow diagram on page 70 to check that your section follows the comparison structure.

Pages 80–81: Planning A Poetry Response

QUICK TEST
1. Comparison of the two poems, specific analysis and terminology, awareness of the relevance of context, a well-structured essay.
2. Planning focuses your thoughts and allows you to produce a well-structured essay.
3. Quotations give you more opportunities to do specific AO2 analysis.

EXAM PRACTICE
Poem choices for comparison would include 'Lines Written in Early Spring', 'Shall earth no more inspire thee', 'In a London Drawingroom', 'A Wider View', 'With Birds You're Never Lonely' and 'A Portable Paradise'. Ideas for the comparison might include positive feelings, negative feelings, how feelings about a place change and how a place can feel like part of someone's identity.

Pages 82–85: Graded Responses

EXAM PRACTICE
Use the mark scheme to self-assess your strengths and weaknesses. Work up from the bottom, putting a tick by things you have fully accomplished, a ½ by skills that are in place but need securing, and underlining areas that need particular development. The estimated grade boundaries are included so you can assess your progress towards your target grade.

Grade	AO1 (12 marks)	AO2 (12 marks)	AO3 (6 marks)
6–7+	A convincing, well-structured essay that answers the question fully. Quotations and references are well-chosen and integrated into sentences. The response provides a detailed and thoughtful comparison of the two poems.	Analysis of the full range of the poets' methods. Thorough exploration of the effects of these methods. Accurate range of subject terminology.	Exploration is linked to specific aspects of the poems' contexts to show a detailed understanding
4–5	A clear essay that always focuses on the exam question. Quotations and references support ideas effectively. The response includes several comparisons.	Explanation of the poets' different methods. Clear understanding of the effects of these methods. Accurate use of subject terminology.	References to relevant aspects of context show a clear understanding.
2–3	The essay has some good comparative ideas that are mostly relevant. Some quotations and references are used to support the ideas.	Identification of some different methods used by the poets to convey meaning. Some subject terminology.	Some awareness of how ideas are affected by the poems' contexts.

Snap up other topic books from Collins:

| 9780008520106 | 9780008520328 | 9780008520335 | 9780008306625 | 9780008306632 |

| 9780008306656 | 9780008306649 | 9780008551506 | 9780008247164 | 9780008247133 |

| 9780008247126 | 9780008551544 | 9780008551537 | 9780008247096 | 9780008551520 |

| 9780008551513 | 9780008551551 | 9780008320096 | 9780008768935 | 9780008520755 |

Browse online at
collins.co.uk/revision